THE HEALER

Also by Leonard Levitt

AN AFRICAN SEASON
THE LONG WAY ROUND

Edited by Leonard Levitt

THE BROTHERS OF ATTICA (by Richard X. Clark)

Leonard Levitt

THE HEALER

The Viking Press / New York

First published in 1980 by The Viking Press
625 Madison Avenue, New York, N.Y. 10022
Published simultaneously in Canada by
Penguin Books Canada Limited

LIBRARY OF CONGRESS CATALOGING IN PUBLICATION DATA
Levitt, Leonard, 1941–
The healer.
1. Friedgood, Charles E.   2. Trials (Poisoning)—New York (State)
3. Surgeons—New York (State)—Biography.   I. Title.
KF224.F74L48   345.747′02523   80-15006
ISBN 0-670-36442-8

Printed in the United States of America
Set in CRT Gael

To Susan Elizabeth

Author's Note

THIS BOOK BEGAN WITH A SERIES OF ARTICLES I wrote as a reporter for the Long Island newspaper *Newsday*. The articles were about a surgeon, Dr. Charles Friedgood, who was convicted of murdering his wife. During the trial the jury heard testimony from three of his four grown daughters. One of the daughters testified she had hidden the needle he had presumedly used to kill his wife. A second daughter was, at the time of her mother's death, suing her for her share of a trust fund the mother had refused to turn over to her as she was legally required to do. A third daughter, with her husband, had alerted the police when her father attempted to flee the country to join his mistress in Denmark. As the trial continued I began interviewing the daughters, trying to make some sense of this family and its tragedy. Three daughters agreed to be interviewed and their interviews formed the basis for the articles, which appeared after Friedgood's conviction.

It was then I began receiving calls from doctors who had trained or practiced with Friedgood. These doctors told an incredible and appalling story, which forms the basis of this book. The picture these doctors painted of Friedgood was that of an able, if not brilliant, surgeon who was nevertheless a pathological liar, unable to tell the truth to his superiors, colleagues, or patients. He had been thrown out of medical school for forging a recommendation. He had lied about his military service. He had inveigled his way back into medical school, then managed to train with some of the nation's foremost surgeons. Yet virtually every hospital he was affiliated with had dismissed him.

From the most prestigious hospitals in New York City, he had descended to the Medicaid mills in the slums, where he treated the poorest, the least educated, the most vulnerable. Because he was kind to them, took time with them, seemed to care for them, his patients idolized him. Tragically, they allowed him to operate on them at whim—he performed ten, fifteen, sometimes twenty operations on the same patient—then on their relatives as well. Other times, he performed operations considered by most surgeons to be unsafe or ineffective. He operated out of his field.

Though he was dismissed by one hospital after another, no written record existed of this, much less of the reasons for his dismissals: doctors, like members of other, vastly different professions—whether they are cops or the capos of organized crime—are taught not to testify formally against each other. Thus the chronicle that exists of Friedgood's career is an oral, off-the-record one, whispered from doctor to doctor. Because no accurate written record was kept he was able to continue to practice. And when he was brought to justice it was not as a result of any action taken by the medical profession, which had known of him for thirty years, but because of the diligence of suburban police officers. Without their persistence, Friedgood would no doubt have gotten away with his wife's murder and would still be practicing. Even now, convicted of murder, he still continues to treat patients—in prison.

Though this book may seem to be an indictment of the

medical profession, or at least of the profession's inability to discipline itself, I would like to make it clear how much help I received from literally scores of doctors who had been as appalled as I was by what Friedgood had been permitted to do to patients over the years. Yet almost all of them have asked for anonymity, lest they run afoul of their colleagues. The code of *omertà*, which is associated with the Mafia, apparently lives as well in more rarefied spheres.

In telling the story of Dr. Charles Friedgood, therefore, it has not always been possible to name names. In a very few cases, the names of peripheral characters in the book have been changed or withheld to protect their privacy, and sources of information have been guaranteed the same kind of anonymity. While most people who provided me with information did not want their names used, some of those I would like to acknowledge are Dr. Milton Virshup of Kings Point, New York, who trained with Charles Friedgood and instructed me on some of the finer points of surgery; Dr. Virshup's wife, Mickey, who was especially helpful in pointing me in the right surgical directions and in encouraging me when the task seemed beyond me; Dr. Leon Canick of Lawrence, New York, who also trained with Friedgood, and Dr. Canick's wife, Alice, who explained something of Friedgood's relationship with his wife, Sophie, at the time they knew them. In addition I would like to thank Marvin Schick of Brooklyn and Rabbi Ronnie Greenwald of Monsey, New York, for directing me to the Hasidic community, and Rabbi Bernard Weinberger for explaining something of Hasidism to me; Nassau County District Attorney Denis Dillon and his assistants Pat Reilly and Barry Grennan, chief of Homicide; Inspector Robert Yaccarino of the Nassau County Police Department; William P. Berry of the Hazelton *Standard-Speaker* and Dr. Norman Wall of Pottstown, Pennsylvania, for giving me background information on Hazelton and the Jewish community in the Pennsylvania coal-mining region; my friends and colleagues, Jim

Willerth of *Time* magazine, Brian Donovan, Dick Zander, and Ken Paul of *Newsday*, and Don Forst of the Boston *Herald-American*, for taking time to read parts of the manuscript; and finally my editor, Amanda Vaill, whose varied—and variegated—education proved invaluable in the preparation of this book.

Contents

Prologue

IT WAS SIX O'CLOCK AND ALREADY DARK ON A COLD December evening in 1976 when the doctor and his attorney got the call and walked back across Old Country Road, through the now-deserted corridors of the Nassau County Court House, and up the three flights of stairs to the courtroom. The jurors were already in their places. The judge, the prosecutor, and the newspaper and television reporters had also arrived, as had a handful of buffs and thrill-seekers who had hung around through the afternoon and into the evening.

"Will the jury please rise?" asked the clerk of the court. "Will the defendant rise and face the jury?"

The doctor stood up—a tall, lean man in his late fifties, with curly gray hair, his eyes steady, unmoving behind his heavy glasses. He turned and faced the jury.

"Mr. Foreman," intoned the clerk, "has the jury reached a verdict?"

"Yes, sir."

"What is the jury's verdict to the first count of murder in the second degree? Guilty or not guilty?"

"We say not . . ." The jury foreman stammered; then began again. "We say . . ."

"What is the jury's verdict to the first count of murder in the second degree?" repeated the clerk. "Guilty or not guilty?"

This time the jury foreman's voice was clear. "We say guilty."

The doctor's jaw dropped. At first, when he heard the word "not," he appeared to smile. Now his shoulders sagged. Yet he uttered not a sound. After that moment when the verdict was announced, his face was expressionless.

The doctor's attorney now asked that the jurors be polled individually. "Members of the jury," the clerk said, "you say you find the defendant Charles E. Friedgood guilty of murder in the second degree. Is that your verdict?" One by one, each juror answered, "Yes."

"Madam and gentlemen, I would like to thank you for the long hours and many weeks and months you worked so diligently," said the judge. "You made a great sacrifice." Suddenly, in the rear of the courtroom, a young woman, as though just comprehending what had occurred moments before, gasped and collapsed, sobbing, into the arms of a man next to her.

Two blue-uniformed court officers, guns at their sides, walked toward the doctor and stood on either side of him; one held out a pair of handcuffs.

The doctor turned and shook hands stiffly, jerkily with his attorney, thanking him, forcing himself to smile. He then reached into his coat pocket and handed the attorney his car keys. The guard put the cuffs on him.

"Thank you," the doctor called, with the same forced smile, to the group of reporters who stood at the door as the guard led him past. "Thank you."

A newspaper account the next day said the doctor had "smiled weakly" as he left the courtroom. Someone else noted that as he walked out the door he seemed to have not a care in the world.

_____ Part I
THE DOCTOR

HE IS KNOWN AS THE GRAND RABBI, PRESENT
descendant of a Hasidic religious line dating back two hundred years and taking its name from a little Russian village
near Kiev, in the Ukraine. Legend has it that an ancestor with
the same surname held court amid "luxury and splendor," as
the *Encyclopedia Judaica* puts it, "sitting on a silver throne
with the words, 'David, King of Israel lives forever' inscribed
in gold," counseling Jewish artists and musicians who came to
see him from far and near. What counsel the Grand Rabbi provided in those days was often medical advice, for although the
rabbis of his line are thought of by their followers as authorities in many things, medicine was always regarded as their
specialty.

Now, two hundred years later, on a decaying street in
the decaying Borough Park section of Brooklyn, New York,
the man who bears the surname of his ancestor is listed in the
Brooklyn telephone directory. Next to the listing is the title
"Grand Rabbi." Like his ancestors, the Grand Rabbi of Brooklyn is considered a medical authority. Six days a week, from
nine in the evening until sometimes three or four in the morning, he offers medical counsel, and it is not uncommon for fol-

lowers seeking his advice to telephone him from all parts of the world. Sometimes in the middle of the night he is able to locate a doctor to perform an emergency operation early the next morning. He even has, it is whispered, the telephone numbers of the doctors' mistresses.

For those who can afford little or nothing for surgery, he can recommend a doctor who will perform the operation for a low fee or even—in rare cases—free of charge. Sometimes he himself will recommend whether a person should undergo surgery.

The Grand Rabbi's home and office are on the second floor of a two-story brick apartment building, which is but a few doors from the *yeshiva* the rabbi heads. The glass in the window of the building's front door has long been missing. The stairway to his apartment creaks. The smell of food seeps out into the hallway. From behind the closed door of the apartment can be heard the squeals of small children.

Inside the door, on a wintry night a year after Dr. Charles Friedgood received the verdict, stands a black-bearded young man in a long black coat. He is one of the Grand Rabbi's acolytes. "You've come to see the rabbi?" he says. "You are lucky. Usually there is a long line. But tonight no one is waiting."

He walks to an adjoining room—the Grand Rabbi's study. Moments later he returns. "The rabbi will see you now," he announces.

The Grand Rabbi is sitting in the corner of the room. He is a middle-aged man, in his late forties or early fifties perhaps, with a florid complexion and flowing red beard. He is wearing a long black coat, and a closet door standing open reveals a row of identical black coats. The Grand Rabbi is seated at a desk with two telephones. The desk is covered with pieces of paper. From among them protrudes a fifty-dollar bill.

The Grand Rabbi neither rises nor shakes hands. The acolyte silently closes the door and stands at a distance by a window overlooking the street. A light snow has begun.

"So you have come to see me about Dr. Friedgood," the Grand Rabbi begins. "I knew him well. He worked around the corner here, at Maimonides Hospital. He was on the surgical staff under Ripstein, then later under Hurwitz.

"A wonderful doctor. A marvelous surgeon. His patients loved him. He was warm, generous, the kindest man on earth. People swore by him. He saw patients at all hours. If they couldn't pay, he operated for free. He wrote letters for people, recommendations, disabilities. If they needed a letter, they went to Dr. Friedgood.

"He could have had anything he wanted," the Grand Rabbi continues, staring out the window at the falling snow. "He could have been the greatest Jewish surgeon in America. He could have had millions. Nobody could surpass him. Money, women, *shiksas*—he could have had anything he wanted."

The Grand Rabbi shakes his head. He belches, then scratches inside his ear with a ballpoint pen. "You know, they threw him out of Maimonides Hospital. Brookdale also. It was called Beth El then. Oh, the doctors there won't talk about it. They won't tell you anything.

"He asked me to intercede with the chief of surgery— with Hurwitz. Hurwitz got angry at me. 'Don't speak to me about Friedgood,' he shouted at me."

The Grand Rabbi pauses. Again he stares out the window into the night and the snow. "You know, he thought he could do anything, Friedgood—heart surgery, stomach, breast, gynecology. . . . He thought he was smarter than anybody else. And he could deceive so easily.

"Where is he now? In prison, you say? For murder? . . . I can believe it. About him I can believe anything. About him anything is possible. You know, the Talmud has a saying: 'Only a fool tells a lie he knows can be discovered.' Friedgood lied so often. And he knew the lies he told would be discovered. I am no psychiatrist, but perhaps that is what he wanted."

The Grand Rabbi rises. The audience is over.

FRIEDGOOD, CHARLES EDWARD. Certified thoracic surgery 1957, surgery 1952. Born 1918 Toledo, Ohio. MSc 1945, MD 1946 (both at Wayne State University, Michigan). Intern (Detroit) 1946–47. Harrison Fellow, Department of Surgery (Pennsylvania) 1947–48. Resident in surgery (Mount Sinai Hospital, New York City) 1948–50. Resident in surgery 1950–52, full-time associate in surgery 1952 (both at Maimonides Hospital, Brooklyn). Resident in thoracic and cardiovascular surgery (both at Hahnemann) 1954. Resident in thoracic surgery (Veterans Hospital, Brooklyn) 1955. Instructor, Department of Anatomy (Wayne) 1944–45, Department of Surgery (Pennsylvania) 1947–48. Assistant professor of surgery (State University of New York, Downstate Medical Center, Brooklyn) 1952. Medical Corps US Army until 1944 . . .

—Adapted from *Directory of Medical Specialists,*
1977–78 edition

ALWAYS THERE WERE THE LIES.

He told his children his father had been an itinerant peddler and that he himself had spent his childhood in the family car as his father traveled with the family from one Midwestern town to the next. Years later, when he was on trial for evading nearly $300,000 in income taxes, he described his father as a wealthy landowner with vast holdings in Israel that his family had owned for generations.

In truth, his past was considerably more prosaic than either of these two tales suggests. His father, Heinrich, or Ichy, as he was called in Yiddish, was born in Poland, immigrated to what was then Palestine, and finally settled in the United States soon after the turn of the century. For the rest of his life he eked out a living in a small clothing store, first in Toledo, Ohio, where his son was born, and later fifty miles away in Detroit, where he moved his family in the 1920s.

It was a meager living at best, selling closeout items to jobbers and discount houses and—when times were especially bad—to housewives, door to door. When the old man retired in 1960, after all the years of buying and selling, his accumulated wealth was but a few thousand dollars.

Ichy's wife, Eva—or, in Yiddish, Chafke—was also an immigrant. A deeply religious woman, she kept a kosher home and was forever reciting from the Bible. Petite, delicate, with blue eyes and milk-white skin, she had been a beautiful woman. An only child, born late in life to parents each in their second marriage, she claimed she had married at sixteen, and in her later years she liked to say she was still so youthful-looking that people often mistook her and her son for brother and sister.

Charles Friedgood did in fact have a younger sister, Shirley, who remained in Detroit, married a dentist, and raised a family, and whose name would come up only at her brother's income-tax trial—when, testifying in his brother-in-law's defense, her husband, the dentist, explained he had willingly invested $40,000 in one of Friedgood's get-rich-quick schemes.

Of all of them it is the mother whose unseen presence

can be felt throughout her son's life. Through it all—the scandals and cover-ups and trials—she, the mother, remained loyal to him, as he, in his own way, did to her.

When the murder trial began and he tried to send the old lady off to Florida to spare her the ordeal, she cried, cajoled, and finally made her way back to him. For a time she lived alone with him in his fourteen-room house, and once a reporter searching for her son came upon her bustling about the house—a small, delicate-looking woman, nearly eighty years old by then. The reporter asked what she felt had brought her son to this tragic end. "Do you know the Bible?" she said, with a trace of an accent. "Do you know the prophet Isaiah? 'I raised my children up to be great and they betrayed me.'" Venomously, the old lady began to speak of her son's children, her grandchildren. "The Bible says, 'Your enemies will come out of your belly,'" she almost spat out. "Those children squealed."

/ ii

Ichy Friedgood settled his family in a four-story apartment building at 11845 LaSalle Boulevard, between Toledo and Elmhurst avenues, across the street from the Roosevelt Elementary–Durfee Junior High–Central High School complex on Detroit's west side. The building is a vacant lot now, bulldozed by urban renewal. The school complex, although still functioning, is decaying and forlorn; the days when the streets around it were closed to summer traffic so that poor neighborhood children had a place to roller-skate are now only a memory.

It was a Jewish neighborhood then, poor but respectable, of two- and four-family houses, and the apartment building at 11845 LaSalle was in the poorest part of all. This was Detroit's second-generation Jewish ghetto, succeeding the one on the city's east side, where the first wave of Jewish immigrants had arrived before World War I, penniless and illiterate in English, to work on Henry Ford's Highland Park assembly line. By the end of the war, as the community grew and prospered, the ghetto spread north, across Grand River, which runs in a loop around the city's downtown, and west across Woodward Avenue, which divides Detroit into east and west.

It was a small and close-knit community, which would never exceed five percent of the population, in a city—and in the industry that dominated it—that would never be particularly hospitable to Jews. In Grosse Pointe, where the auto kings, the Fords and Dodges, lived, Jews would be barred as late as the 1960s. Even then the village initiated a "point system," rating prospective homeowners on such factors as place of birth. When asked whether this amounted to discrimination, one of the no doubt more enlightened residents replied he was certain Albert Einstein would have qualified for residence.

It would be through education, through Central High, from which Charles Friedgood graduated in 1936, that many of Detroit's Jews would rise, though they would never fully be accepted in Detroit. Central, which drew the poor Jews near the school and the rich Jews who lived farther north in the mansions on Boston and Chicago boulevards, would become the jewel of the city's school system. Central would send more of its graduates to college, graduate the highest percentage to the University of Michigan in Ann Arbor, and produce more PhDs, it was said, than any other high school in the state. Years later, one of them, a scientist who had graduated from Central with Friedgood, said that no matter where he had studied or worked, in college, in graduate school, in his profession, he had never worked harder than at Central. And what was so remarkable about Charles Friedgood and his classmates from Central was how many succeeded, in business, law, academe, and medicine—and how many felt compelled years later to change their Jewish names.

/ iii

Those who remember Chuck Friedgood, as he called himself in Central High, remember a bright, extremely handsome young man, lean-featured, with blond hair and a charming smile. He was a fellow of jaunty confidence, who seemed to walk on the balls of his feet; who ran on the cross-country team; who was something of a health fetishist, carrying a bag of carrots and celery with him to school; and who, like all other poor students at Central, worked almost every day after school, delivering newspapers or helping in his father's clothing store.

There is a photograph of Charles Friedgood, taken in 1935, in his junior year, in the school yearbook, *The Centralite,* with its outline of the school's exterior indented on its dark-green cover; its tiresome motto ("Upon Us Rests the Future"); its dedication to a Miss Eloise André, a gray-haired spinster garbed in black, beneath whose picture appear the words "Who since 1896 has communicated the language of love and nature to students of Central." Friedgood—the photograph is overexposed, turning his blond hair dark—appears in a group shot of the school's cross-country team. It shows him in white track shorts and a sleeveless shirt with a block letter *C,* a lanky, good-looking boy who confronts the camera with a faint, enigmatic smile.

Despite his looks, despite his intelligence, despite his confidence, there was something about Chuck Friedgood that kept people at a distance. There was the year he had dropped out of school, about which he never spoke. It was whispered he had had tuberculosis, a dreaded disease then. Treatable, curable, it nonetheless left its victims with some career doors closed to them, careers that included medicine. Then there was his aloofness, which was more than mere reserve. There was a roguishness, almost an amorality—a word used over the years to describe him. "He was someone I instinctively stayed away from," recalled Robert Luby, who ran cross-country with him and who is now director of athletics for the Detroit public schools.

Edward Rosen was also on that cross-country team. Although he went on to become a biochemist, an eminent man in his field, and though he never saw Chuck Friedgood again after college, Edward Rosen would never forget him. Unable to afford the tuition at the University of Michigan, Friedgood and Rosen attended Wayne State University, the respectable urban college where students saved money by living at home. It was there, at Wayne, Rosen remembered years later, "that the strange streaks in Chuck began to show up."

Though Friedgood was a pre-med student, he never, Rosen remembered, seemed to do any work. "He always had more leisure time than the rest of us. I don't know if he ever studied seriously. Lord knows how many times he cheated."

In their second year at Wayne, Rosen recalled, he and Friedgood took a course together, a quantitative-chemistry lab with a Professor Edward J. Bird, one of the school's old-timers. Bird gave the students a number of different solutions whose identity and composition they didn't know. The student had to analyze each solution to determine the identity and precise quantity of each component and then enter his calculations in an individual Unknown Book. Bird kept the identity of each student's unknowns in a notebook hidden in a desk drawer in his office.

It was a difficult course, one demanding rigorous research and perseverance. Half the student's grade was determined by the final exam, the other half by the analytical calculations in his Unknown Book. Friedgood, however, rarely showed up in the laboratory. By exam time, said Rosen, Friedgood "was desperate."

A few days before the final, Friedgood approached Rosen with a startling proposition. The night before, he boasted, he had gone to Bird's office. Bird and the other professors had long since left for the day, and only a night watchman was on duty. Friedgood had brought with him a bottle of cheap wine, which he handed to the watchman. As the watchman moved off, Friedgood climbed up over the transom into Bird's office and found the professor's notebook with the list of unknowns.

Rosen was incredulous. Was Friedgood kidding? He had barely attended Bird's lab. How could he know exactly where the notebook was hidden?

Friedgood then proudly offered to provide Rosen with the answers to *his* unknowns. Rosen was appalled. "You can just go to hell," he answered, and walked away.

Undaunted, during the final exam Friedgood made certain to take a seat next to Rosen, then proceeded to copy answers from him throughout the exam. As for the unknowns, Friedgood wrote his calculations correct to the third decimal point, something no student had been able to do in twenty-five years.

Despite his misgivings about Friedgood, Rosen remained friends with him. Why, Rosen never fully understood. "He clung to me," he would explain years later. "He seemed to have an affinity for me precisely because I had a conscience, because honesty and integrity were qualities that were important to me." And the straitlaced Rosen, like the eminent surgeons who later befriended Friedgood, appeared amused, if not fascinated, by Friedgood's lack of honesty and integrity.

The aloofness people had sensed about Friedgood at Central High became more pronounced now at Wayne. Though he was the handsomest one of them, Rosen remembered, and totally self-assured, Rosen and his friends often remarked that they never saw Charlie Friedgood with a girl. Instead, on Saturday nights he often approached his friends and suggested, "Come on, let's go downtown and crash some hotel parties and roll some drunks."

Rosen and the others would stare at each other, perplexed. Then, after Friedgood had gone off by himself, they would say that Charlie had just been kidding, boasting in that roguish way he had. Years later, however, Rosen could not get such incidents out of his mind. "He talked about rolling drunks so often. Always so matter-of-factly. God knows we all needed the money. But somehow we always told ourselves he was just kidding."

Rosen and Friedgood also joined a debating society, which was considered great sport then. It was called the Philomathic Oratorical Society, a prestigious debating group that met Sundays in a synagogue classroom. Many prominent local attorneys and judges had been members of the society, and much research went into the debates. But as in Bird's chemistry lab, what astonished Rosen was that although Friedgood never did any research, he still—with total self-assurance—was always able to demolish his opponent's case, using quotes and citing page references.

Once, after one of Friedgood's better performances, Rosen asked to see his references. "Charlie just laughed. The references, the pages, the quotes—he made them all up."

The culmination of the society's activity each year was an oratory contest open to everyone, the subjects chosen by the participants, the winner to receive a gold medal. These contests were held in the auditorium of a local high school, and parents and attorneys throughout the city attended. "I never had the guts to enter," Rosen remembered. "But one year Charlie volunteered." Why Friedgood entered, Rosen never understood. He did not seem to have a particular subject in mind. Nor did he bother to prepare. Instead, as the contest approached and Rosen repeatedly asked him what his subject was, Friedgood continued to say he did not know.

The night of the contest, Rosen remembered, Friedgood called him. After dinner the two took the bus together to Northern High School, where the contest was to be held. On the bus, again Rosen asked what Friedgood's subject was.

"Charlie, what are you going to talk about?" Rosen said.

"I don't know," Friedgood replied.

"But don't you *know?*" Rosen pressed him. "Don't you have any idea?"

Friedgood, Rosen recalled, just shrugged. Even as Friedgood walked to the stage, it appeared to Rosen he hadn't made up his mind. "By now," Rosen remembered, "I'm quaking. Here comes his turn." Suddenly, as Rosen watched, dumbstruck, his friend Charlie Friedgood began giving an impassioned speech about Palestine, "a strange, illogical mixture," Rosen remembered, "with him shouting and waving his arms. There were many Jewish people in the audience. When Charlie finished, they were in tears." All those people who had prepared so assiduously, Rosen thought to himself, and Charlie won the gold medal.

Then, as Friedgood walked off the stage, he ignored the crowd of people approaching him, all trying to congratulate him. Instead he walked straight up to Rosen, smiled, and said simply, "See?"

/ iv

In 1940 Friedgood was accepted at the prestigious University of Michigan medical school. Rosen was also accepted at Ann Arbor, as a doctoral candidate in chemistry. He married, had Friedgood over to dinner once, then never saw him again.

But he never forgot Charlie Friedgood. Years later, after he had moved to the West Coast, changed his name, and become the head of biochemistry at a prestigious hospital outside Los Angeles, and another Central High cross-country teammate had become a dean at one of the University of California medical schools, the two often reflected on their days in Detroit at Central High. They remembered how poor they had both been, how hard they had had to work, how envious they had been of the richer students who lived on Boston and Chicago boulevards, who had been as bright as they but had not had to struggle as they had done.

Invariably, as they talked, the conversation would turn to Charlie Friedgood. The medical-school dean would recall how Friedgood had sold other students clothes from his father's store, "clothes that never seemed to last out a rainstorm." He also recalled that once Friedgood had sold a well-built shot-putter a sports jacket that had shrunk the first time it was cleaned. He remembered the shot-putter's holding Friedgood up against a locker and shaking him until Friedgood agreed to return his money.

"And his character never changed," the dean would say to Rosen as the years went by and stories of Friedgood's medical career filtered back to them. "How could someone who made so many waves, who was in trouble at every stage of his life, go as far as he did?"

Rosen had no answers. He himself was increasingly disturbed by what he remembered of his old classmate. "Here was a guy," Rosen said, "with no conscience. A true sociopath. As a biochemist, I would find myself wondering if there was not actually something wrong with the way Friedgood's brain was structured. Whenever I thought of him, I would find myself thinking of Leopold and Loeb."

What disturbed Rosen most was that he himself had done nothing to stop him. "It was a case of charm winning over integrity," he explained. "He was just so charming. And I guess all of us were simply looking the other way when we saw those early signs of pathology.

"I know now I should have stopped him. I should have blown the whistle on him. When he got the answers to that chemistry lab and offered them to me, I told him to go to hell, but I should have turned him in."

Later, in his own career, Rosen would be faced with similar situations, with scientists who falsified results. "Science can only operate with faith and integrity," he said, "and whenever you see the opposite you must wipe it out."

Yet each time he was tempted to turn these people in, he didn't. "I would think, There people have families, children. Should I do this to someone and ruin his career? So, each time I would pass the buck. I would write a letter of recommendation in which I did not say what the trouble was. And so the problem just got bigger and bigger.

"With Friedgood, people all along the way were faced with this question and all of us answered the wrong way. We were all accomplices. I remember when I found out Charlie Friedgood was a surgeon my first thought was about all the horrible things he could do to people. . . ."

3

CHARLES FRIEDGOOD NEVER GRADUATED FROM the University of Michigan medical school. In his last year there, he was expelled.

In his next to last year he had been forced to leave school temporarily because the tuberculosis had recurred. When he returned for his senior year and applied to internship programs, he tried to keep his tuberculosis off his record; just as he had climbed into Professor Bird's office at Wayne, he now stole personal stationery from Michigan's respected dean of medicine, Dr. Fred Coller. On it he wrote recommendations for himself, testifying above Coller's forged signature that he was in excellent health.

And just as on Bird's laboratory final he had given remarkably accurate answers, he now gave himself recommendations that surpassed anything Coller had ever written for anyone else. Because they were unique, a doctor at one of the hospitals to which Friedgood had applied wrote back to Coller, thanking him for recommending such an outstanding individual as Charles Friedgood.

There is no written record of Coller's reply.

Years later, when he was asked about his expulsion from

Michigan, Friedgood would smile and shrug. "They said I had tuberculosis. I didn't. We disagreed. I was expelled."

Michigan's terse explanation, which, ironically, proved prescient, was merely "psychological reasons."

/ ii

Charles Friedgood was expelled in 1944. With the country at war, all graduating medical students had to enter the army as second lieutenants. Those who had not graduated had to join as privates. But what happened to Charles Friedgood the year he left Michigan is a mystery. Years later he would list himself in the *Directory of Medical Specialists* as having served in the Army Medical Corps during 1944. Yet how he was able to enter the army with tuberculosis, where he served, why and when he was discharged while the war continued—these questions remain unanswered, for the United States Army has no record of Charles Friedgood's having served at all.

Toward the end of 1944, however, Sidney Miller—a former classmate of Friedgood's at Wayne and at that time a student at Wayne's medical school—bumped into him on a street in Detroit. Thirty-five years later, Miller, an obstetrician in Detroit, remembered the meeting. Friedgood informed Miller that he was out of the army. His unit had had orders to go overseas but he had received a medical discharge.

With that, Friedgood took a letter from his pocket. It was, Miller remembered, from Fitzsimmons Army Hospital in Denver, signed by a colonel, the hospital's chief of orthopedics. Friedgood, the chief had written, was the best medical corpsman he had ever seen. He knew more about orthopedics than anyone else the chief had ever met.

Years later Fitzsimmons Hospital could find no records on Charles Friedgood.

Only a few months later, Miller received another surprise. He was taking a laboratory course in histology—the study of tissues—and one day he walked into his lab to find Charlie Friedgood installed as the new laboratory research assistant. The histology lab was run by Warren Nelson, a kindly professor and a recognized figure in histology, who would become the first medical director of John D. Rockefeller III's World Population Council. At Wayne he was one of a triumvirate of deans who unofficially ran the school, and would become the first of many prominent medical figures to aid Friedgood's career.

"I don't know when Nelson fell in love with Chuck," recalled Fred Dalton, then a medical student at Wayne and now a psychiatrist on Long Island and the head of the school's alumni association, "but he certainly became his champion."

To Nelson, Friedgood was the victim of an injustice. "I know what he did at Ann Arbor," Dalton overheard Nelson say to another professor. "But he has been punished and paid the price; he should be given another chance."

In Nelson's lab Friedgood—though only a technician and not an enrolled student—was placed in charge of the laboratory animals, and with a team of medical students he began experiments to induce diabetes in guinea pigs. In most cases an animal is prepared for such a study by the removal of its pancreas, which produces insulin. In guinea pigs, however, there are no clear cleavage lines between the pancreas and other organs, and scientists use a process called chemical ablation, which destroys the Islets of Langerhans—cells in the pancreas that secrete the insulin.

Friedgood's series of tests on the guinea pigs lasted nearly two years, during which time his group produced a number of papers that discussed Friedgood's results. Dean Nelson was impressed, and in 1945 he persuaded the admissions committee to admit Friedgood into the senior year of medical school.

Later, students reviewing the results of Friedgood's experiments would be unable to corroborate his findings.

/ iii

But he was a medical student again. He was older now, a few years older than the other med students. He cultivated a slim mustache. He was well dressed, in a dapper sort of way. He was well mannered and soft-spoken and completely self-assured. To the younger medical students he conveyed a sense of maturity. One of them, Harry Lewis, now a surgeon himself, remembered: "We had seen him in our anatomy lab, but we didn't know much about him. He was a little different, a little *apart*, somehow. We had all heard he had had some trouble at Michigan. He was a little older. He never had any money. And we went out of our way to include him in everything we did. He was good-looking, bright as hell, mature. We felt he had the makings of something great." Harry Lewis drove an old Dodge and liked to pick up his friends each morning on the way to school. Since he passed Friedgood's parents' apartment on LaSalle on his way to Wayne, Lewis began picking up Charlie Friedgood, too.

And so Friedgood became part of Lewis' circle of friends, a small group of Jewish medical students who partied and made weekend excursions together and joined a Jewish medical fraternity—all except Friedgood, who couldn't afford to pay the dues. Still, the others made a point of inviting him to their Saturday-night fraternity parties, and he came regularly. But, they noticed, he kept to himself. After a few drinks, they would become boisterous, laughing, shouting, telling dirty jokes to one another. All except Charlie Friedgood. Whenever they told dirty jokes around him, they felt uncomfortable.

Often after these Saturday-night parties there would be leftover sandwiches, and Harry Lewis would take them and place them in the back seat of his Dodge for lunch at school the following Monday. One Monday, after he had picked up Friedgood, Lewis noticed the sandwiches had disappeared. "I never said anything to Chuck about it—he never had any money, so I just figured. . . ." Instead, each Monday, Lewis made sure to leave the sandwiches on the back seat. And every Monday morning after he picked up Friedgood they were gone.

Harry Lewis had a cousin, Rose Davidson, who had married into one of the richest Jewish families in Detroit. Her husband, one of three Davidson brothers, had made his fortune in the Depression when he and his brothers bought up a number of failing warehouses that they turned into a chain known as Federal Department Stores. By World War II, Federal Department Stores had become the largest discount chain in Detroit, and Rose Davidson and her husband could afford a large house on Boston Boulevard, where some of the wealthiest families in Detroit lived. They also had an elegant summer estate north of Detroit on Pine Lake. Rose's elder daughter had married a surgeon and now Rose was casting about for a prospect for her younger daughter, Geraldine. During the semester break she invited her cousin Harry Lewis to bring some of his med-school friends up for a weekend at the lake. It was an invitation Lewis and the Davidson family would soon regret.

In the summer of 1945 Lewis, Friedgood, and two other young men drove up to the lake in Lewis' Dodge. The Davidson house sat atop a hill, at the end of a long driveway bounded on either side by forests, with a great lawn sloping down to the lake, where a boathouse, a dock, and the Davidsons' large white Chris-Craft sat. As the young medical students came up the drive toward the house they fell silent—struck by the estate's beauty, the large trees overhanging the driveway, the freshly cut lawn that seemed to run on endlessly down to the water. Lewis turned around in his seat to his friend Chuck Friedgood. Friedgood, Lewis remembered, was staring out the window, his eyes wide.

They stopped at the front door of the house, which was surrounded by an enclosed porch. Before they could step from

the car, a black butler appeared to take their luggage. Again
Lewis turned to Friedgood. Friedgood's mouth hung open
and he appeared unable to speak. "I thought," Lewis remembered, "Chuck would faint."

He recovered enough to greet his hosts, and their
daughter, with his usual easy charm. Geraldine Davidson was
in her early twenties, a tall, large-boned girl—not Chuck's
type at all, Lewis remembered thinking. Yet all that weekend
Lewis and the others saw little of their friend. When they did
see him, he was playing tennis with Geraldine, or out on the
lake, standing next to her at the wheel of the Chris-Craft. He
seemed so nonchalant, so sure of himself. "What amazed us
all," said Lewis, "was that Chuck knew every move. He acted
as though he had been playing tennis and handling a boat all
his life." Two months later Friedgood and Geraldine were engaged.

They were married in December 1945 at one of Detroit's best downtown hotels. With the war over and luxury
goods no longer scarce, there was the best of everything at
the wedding—food, wines, champagne. During the wedding
Friedgood seemed to be everywhere, holding hands with Geraldine, hugging and kissing all the guests, running up to Lewis, throwing his arms around him and calling him "cousin."

Yet, after the wedding, Lewis did not see much of his
old friend anymore. Chuck Friedgood moved from his parents' apartment on LaSalle into Geraldine's home on Boston
Boulevard. Instead of hitching rides in Lewis' Dodge, he now
drove to medical school in a new convertible.

Then, one morning, as the med students were arriving
for class, a black chauffeured limousine pulled up to the curb.
The students all stopped and stared, wondering who the important person in the limousine was. As they gaped, out of the
back seat stepped Chuck Friedgood. As he had during his
high-school health-fetish days, he was carrying a gigantic bag
filled with carrots, celery, and pickles, which that afternoon in
the cafeteria at lunch he proceeded to pass out to everyone.

"We all made big jokes about the car," recalls Fred Dalton, the Long Island psychiatrist. "We kidded Chuck that he had married Geraldine for her money and that he would never have to work again. To us it was like a dream come true for him. We all wanted to marry someone like that. But none of us ever did except him."

/ iv

But there were problems with the marriage that were soon apparent to everyone. "He was just too fast," recalled Lewis. "He did everything with Geraldine too fast. It was all too obvious."

Soon after the wedding Friedgood began outfitting himself with new gabardine suits, silk ties, and new shoes from Hughes & Hatcher, the toniest men's shop in Detroit, charging the bills to the Davidson family account. He also began outfitting his parents, Ichy and Chafke, there, charging their clothes to the Davidsons as well.

To his fellow students at Wayne, he seemed always to be showing off his clothes and convertible. Not to lord it over them, they felt, but, rather, merely to show them. "Look what I've got!" he would say. "Isn't it wonderful?" "But never," Lewis recalled, "did he say, 'Isn't Geraldine's family wonderful? Isn't Geraldine wonderful?' "

Then, one day, Friedgood went too far. At the time, the board of directors of Federal Department Stores consisted only of Davidson family members—Geraldine's father and his two brothers—but Friedgood, as one of the family, felt he should attend as well. And so at the next board meeting he simply appeared. As he entered the room the Davidson brothers looked up. Conversation stopped.

"What are you doing here, Chuck?" his father-in-law asked, perplexed.

"I'm here because I want to know where I fit in," said Friedgood.

There was a pause. Then one of his wife's uncles stood up. "I'll tell you where you fit in," he announced. And led Friedgood out the door.

The marriage lasted less than two years, during which time Friedgood was graduated from Wayne and did his internship at Detroit Receiving Hospital. In the meantime his old crowd had dispersed, and Harry Lewis had been graduated from Wayne and left Detroit for an internship in Philadelphia. Lewis hadn't heard from any of them in some time when Chuck Friedgood telephoned.

"I'm in town looking for a house," he said. "I've been offered a residency in surgery at the University of Pennsylvania with Ravdin."

Lewis was impressed—Isidor Ravdin was the most eminent surgeon in the country then. "Gerry must be thrilled," he said. "How is she, by the way?"

"Oh, fine," Friedgood answered. "She'll be coming here soon."

A few hours later Lewis received another phone call. It was from a friend, Richard Gimbel, whose family owned the Gimbel department store in Philadelphia. Gimbel's daughter Ann had been at Lewis' graduation ceremony at Wayne and—it now appeared—Friedgood, then married six months, had seen her there.

"Do you have a friend, Chuck Friedgood?" Gimbel asked Lewis. "He told us he was interested in Ann and that he was your friend. We invited him out for the weekend."

Because of that phone call, it was a weekend date Friedgood never kept.

/ v

Five years later Harry Lewis was a struggling young surgeon, attending an American College of Surgeons convention in New York, when he bumped into Charlie Friedgood again.

Friedgood appeared overjoyed at seeing his old friend. "I'm doing great. I'm remarried. I have a great job. I'm doing open-heart surgery," he told Lewis. "And I think this calls for a celebration." Friedgood suggested they all go out to dinner—Lewis, his wife, himself, and his new wife. "I'll make the arrangements," he said.

The restaurant Friedgood chose was Toots Shor. The meal, Lewis recalled, was excellent. But when the waiter brought the check, Friedgood suddenly looked inside his coat, then turned to Lewis.

"Gee," he said. "I'm terribly sorry, but I left my wallet at home."

Lewis was stuck for the bill.

He saw Friedgood only once more after that. Five years later, after Friedgood had been dismissed from one hospital after another, he contacted Lewis and asked him to write a letter of recommendation for him to his surgical chief. Despite all that had gone on before with Friedgood, Lewis had difficulty saying no. He had never forgotten the times Friedgood had taken the sandwiches from the back seat of his car to save money for lunch. I don't approve of what he did, Lewis thought, Chuck took advantage of everyone. Yet at the same time Lewis felt he understood what Friedgood had gone through. Call it compassion, he told himself. Maybe that was why Lewis had become a doctor. He couldn't kick someone when he was down.

In the end, though, Lewis never wrote the letter. It was his wife, he remembers, who persuaded him not to. He never heard from Friedgood again.

As for Geraldine Davidson, she remained in Detroit, remarried, and reared five children. Of her marriage to Friedgood she would never talk, not even to members of her own family. "She was always sensitive about it," her older sister, who had married the surgeon, would say years afterward. "She would never tell us anything. After what happened later, I guess she was lucky."

4

THE FATHER OF MODERN AMERICAN SURGERY WAS
William Stewart Halsted. Brilliant, egocentric, autocratic, bizarre, he dominated his contemporaries and left his mark on
three generations of American surgeons. Born to an old New
York family in 1852, he attended Andover and Yale, studied
medicine in Germany and then in Austria under Theodor Bill-
roth, perhaps the best-known surgeon of his time. In the 1880s
Halsted returned to New York and joined the staffs of two of
the city's oldest hospitals, Bellevue and Roosevelt. His biogra-
pher, W. C. MacCullan, would describe these years as Halsted's "New York period."

At the height of his reputation in New York, his person-
ality seemed to change, for reasons that were not revealed un-
til fifty years after his death. Suddenly Halsted left New York.
From his former mentor at Bellevue, William Welch, he ac-
cepted a position as professor of surgery at Johns Hopkins, in
Baltimore. "A strangely altered man," in MacCullan's words,
Halsted remained at Hopkins until his death thirty years later.
Under his guidance, and that of Welch and William Osler,
Hopkins became the foremost school of medicine and surgery
in the country; it developed the prototype of the residency

system as it exists today and trained a generation of residents who later became heads of surgical departments of the country's leading medical schools.

To his subordinates at Hopkins, Halsted was a harsh disciplinarian. His residents were expected to be on call seven days and nights a week. Because of this they were forbidden to marry, a practice that became common in the profession and continued for the next thirty years. Halsted was also a remote man, and in fact spent the rest of his professional life avoiding patients, students, and the local medical profession. He operated only rarely and demanded enormous fees, once charging a patient of Osler's ten thousand dollars for a gallbladder operation.

Nor was his behavior any less bizarre outside of surgery. A fastidious dresser, he insisted on sending his clothes to Europe to be cleaned. With his wife, the former Caroline Hampton—earlier his operating-room nurse—he vacationed on his South Carolina estate, which he named after his ancestral home in England, High Halsted. Having no children, the two were devoted to their dogs and horses. As H. L. Mencken, who knew him, wrote, they "led a strange sequestered life in a great big house where each had his own quarters and neither saw anybody."

In his later years Halsted suffered repeatedly from severe chest and abdominal pains. Doctors thought he had angina pectoris, a heart condition, but he refused to be examined, consulting only with his old friend Welch. Finally, in 1919 he agreed to allow one of his own residents to operate on him for trouble with his gallbladder—his mother had suffered from the same condition, and Halsted had operated on her for it when she was in her eighties.

Unfortunately the resident left a stone in the common duct and Halsted developed jaundice. Three years later he was operated on again. The stone was removed but pneumonia set in. Shortly thereafter Halsted died. The year was 1922.

All his personal data were placed in a sealed container,

not to be opened for fifty years. And so it was only in 1972 that his secret was revealed: for most of his life Halsted had been a drug addict.

He had become addicted at Bellevue when he self-administered cocaine repeatedly to test it for use as an anesthetic. Unable to cure himself, he had twice, unsuccessfully, institutionalized himself, then moved to Baltimore. In Osler's handwriting was found a notation that Halsted had cut down the dosage of his drug from three to one and a half grams daily. "As of 1912 and possibly afterwards," wrote Osler, "he had possibly gotten on without it."

/ ii

There was a Halsted legacy that—strictly speaking—had little to do with the practice of medicine, but that would nonetheless affect the course of American surgery. Whether or not Halsted himself was an anti-Semite, as his assistants became the heads of the country's surgical departments, Jews, with rare exceptions, were barred from all of them.

Unable to train in surgery in the best hospitals, they were forced to start residency programs of their own. Perhaps the foremost was at Mount Sinai in New York, whose surgical chiefs were regarded by their assistants as eminences no less grand than Halsted himself. There was the great A. A. Berg, who had pioneered, as therapy for a duodenal ulcer, the then revolutionary partial or subtotal gastrectomy—in which two thirds of the stomach is removed in order to stop production of excess stomach acids. This was an operation that had first been criticized in America, then only reluctantly accepted, by the Mayo brothers and Frank Leahy of Boston, who came to Mount Sinai to watch Berg perform it. Even in his eighties, and long past his prime, Berg was permitted to operate at Mount Sinai on his private patients, startling residents with flashes of his former brilliance—and, it was said, by refusing to give patients the postoperative painkilling drug Demerol.

Then there were Berg's successors, and rivals, Colp and Garlock. Garlock had trained at New York Hospital—perhaps the strongest fortress of anti-Semitism—under Poole. Poole so respected Garlock that he chose the young Jewish surgeon to operate on his own wife. Yet feelings against Jews were so strong at New York Hospital that Garlock finally decided he might be better off—as Poole had suggested to him, putting it as charitably as possible—uptown at Mount Sinai "with your own people."

At Mount Sinai, however, Garlock encountered a rival, Colp. That rivalry would split Mount Sinai's surgical department. Though Garlock was clearly the greater surgeon, Colp had his adherents and there would be heated arguments comparing the two. It was said that Colp could perform a mastectomy—an operation Halsted had perfected—in eighteen minutes, that Garlock could perform a complete gastrectomy, skin-to-skin, in thirty-five minutes—a procedure he once demonstrated before an annual meeting of the American College of Surgeons.

Ironically, it was whispered that it was Garlock's shortcomings as a surgical head—certainly not a fault in his technical skill, which was unsurpassed—that led to his death. His ego—the equal of Halsted's—would not allow him to pay his assistants properly. Serving under him, he felt, should be reward enough. As a result, the most competent assistants, it was said, left Mount Sinai to practice elsewhere. The lesser remained. When Garlock suffered an abdominal aortic aneurysm—a blow-out of the main artery that carries blood from the heart to the rest of the body—an assistant misdiagnosed it. Garlock died before ever reaching the operating table.

/ iii

It was into this narrow universe of ego, brilliance, eccentricity, and prejudice that Charles Friedgood sought entry. And improbable as it might seem, in a world whose doors were locked to all but the most brilliant of Jews, Charles Friedgood—already once expelled from one medical school—managed to secure the key.

When Friedgood went to do his residency at the University of Pennsylvania, he was studying under a man considered the foremost American surgeon of his time. Isidor Ravdin was elected president of the American College of Surgeons, the first—and the last—person of Jewish origin to be accorded that honor. When President Eisenhower required abdominal surgery, Ravdin was the physician summoned as a civilian consultant to the army surgeon who did the operation.

Born of German-Jewish parents in 1894 in Evansville, Indiana, Ravdin had come to the University of Pennsylvania Hospital as a medical student in 1918. An exceedingly short man, under five feet tall, he had married the daughter of the chancellor of the university, a Main Line Episcopalian, a head taller than he, and had converted to Episcopalianism. Despite his conversion, and the fact that he traveled in his wife's upper-class circles, Ravdin was, as a contemporary put it, "not unkind to Jewish causes." He was chief of surgery and director of Surgical Research at the University of Pennsylvania Hospital for twenty-five years, and his residency program was one of the few that accepted Jewish students.

Exactly how Charles Friedgood came to study with Ravdin is, like so many other events surrounding Friedgood's medical career, a mystery. Perhaps it is only a coincidence that his ex-sister-in-law's surgeon-husband was a close friend of Ravdin's. A letter in Ravdin's file indicates that a residency was offered to Friedgood in October 1946, while he was interning at Detroit Receiving Hospital and still married to Geraldine. Ravdin's records show that Friedgood was a resident under him for a year—from April 1947 to April 1948.

Yet Friedgood's residency was not renewed. The circumstances under which he and Ravdin parted are not known. The only hint is provided by a letter Ravdin sent to Memorial Hospital in New York when Friedgood applied there in 1949 and gave Ravdin as a reference. In his letter Ravdin says only that Friedgood trained at the University of Pennsylvania Hospital under him for a year. Nothing more. Nothing less.

But for Charles Friedgood, his association with Ravdin, brief as it was and however it had ended, proved invaluable. Because of it, he was accepted into a surgical residency program at Mount Sinai in 1948. Then, in the postwar years, Mount Sinai was at the height of its reputation. The head of its thoracic-surgery department was the eminent Harold "Skippy" Neuhof, and it was to him that Friedgood gravitated. Like Warren Nelson in Detroit, and Ravdin after him, Skippy Neuhof would play an important role in Friedgood's career.

Short and wiry, Neuhof was consumed with boundless energy, and ideas seemed to skip from his head at the rate of a hundred per minute—hence his nickname. To his subordinates Skippy Neuhof could be difficult, if not fearsome. If, however, a resident wished to discuss a patient with him, Neuhof could be called upon at any hour of the night. But if he felt a resident did not measure up, he could be brutal.

Of the surgical residents, the one who appeared to be least overwhelmed by Neuhof was Charles Friedgood. After only a few weeks at Mount Sinai, Friedgood would confidently approach Neuhof in the corridor as a *landsman,* or countryman, and the two of them would walk off together, with Friedgood speaking to Neuhof in Yiddish.

"In the godlike atmosphere Mount Sinai had in those days, with those exalted eminences," a resident with Friedgood would recall years later, "to see Charlie Friedgood *schmeicheling* with Neuhof in Yiddish"—toadying to him—"as though they were old friends—it was too much."

Among the residents, Friedgood was soon referred to as "Neuhof's boy." And with Skippy Neuhof's recommendation he was able to make his next advance in surgery—a surgical residency program at Brooklyn's Maimonides Hospital. From then on—after his year with Ravdin, his two years at Mount Sinai, and his years at Maimonides—no matter how poor his work, no matter how many hospitals dismissed him, those who sought to justify Dr. Charles Friedgood would describe him, as did one hospital administrator, as "having the best training a surgeon can have."

5

BEFORE HE WENT FROM MOUNT SINAI TO MAIMONI-
des, in 1948, a year after his divorce, Friedgood married again.
Sophie Davidowitz was to become the mother of his children,
the woman with whom he would spend the next twenty-eight
years. Like all others whose lives he touched, she would be
hurt by him. In the end the hurt proved fatal.

On the surface they appeared to have much in common. Like Friedgood's, her parents, Hyman and Rose Davidowitz—or Davidovitz, as Hyman sometimes spelled it—
were Jewish immigrants from Eastern Europe. Like Friedgood's parents, they had arrived in America in the early part
of the century and settled in a place where Jews were a small
and never fully accepted minority, the coal-mining town of
Hazleton, Pennsylvania. Yet there was a difference, and in the
end it was this difference that mattered most to Charles Friedgood. Unlike Friedgood's father, who had struggled all his life
and managed to accumulate but a few thousand dollars, Sophie's father was, like the father of Friedgood's former wife, a
millionaire.

With his wife, Rose, and four children, Hyman Davidowitz had come to Hazleton in 1930. The town had been founded a century before, in the early 1800s, when it was discovered that it sat on top of a rich vein of anthracite coal that ran south from Scranton and through the center of the state. For the next hundred years the coal mines dominated the region's economy. Their owners, some of America's first families, imported Welsh immigrants to operate the mines, and they in turn imported immigrant labor—Irish, Italians, and Poles—to go down into them.

The Jews did not arrive in the region until the end of the nineteenth century. They had come first as peddlers, making the trip, as Davidowitz would some thirty years later, west from New York, across New Jersey, and into the foothills of the Poconos, their wares carried on their backs. By then the social hierarchy of the coal towns, with their rickety wooden company houses, had long been established. The Jews found themselves socially ostracized. Barred from the professions and unwilling to go down into the mines, they became instead merchants and tradesmen. They built homes and shops around their synagogues, whose incongruous one- and two-room remnants can still be seen in the nearby coal towns of Shamokin, Frackville, Delano, and Mahanoy City.

By 1930, when Davidowitz arrived in Hazleton, coal mining had already begun to decline, and light industry was entering the area. Hyman Davidowitz, who as a Jew had no place in the mines, managed instead to build up a small shoe factory, the Columbia Slipper Company, and by selling shoes to the army during World War II, he made a fortune.

Still, despite his wealth, there remained something simple and unpretentious, almost humble, about the man. Both he and his wife, Rose, never lost their heavy European accents. They made sure their children all learned to read both Yiddish and Hebrew. And they never seemed to care whether the last syllable of their name—"-witz"—was spelled with a *w*, as it was printed in the local paper, or with a *v*, the way it appeared on his tombstone.

Late in life, after he had married off his three daughters and his son had taken over the factory, he became president of Hazleton's synagogue and helped pay off its mortgage. An account in the local paper at the time described him as "the outsider who taught the community how to give."

Then, in 1960, he bequeathed to the Jewish community a gift of a twenty-acre camp, with cabins and a lake, which was named, in perhaps the only outward indulgence he would allow himself, Camp Davidowitz. There is a picture of him at the dedication ceremony, which was attended by all leaders of Hazleton's Jewish community. The picture shows him and his wife inspecting a cabin. The old man is standing at the door, in baggy pants and a sports shirt, and he is gazing admiringly, but at the same time almost unbelievingly, at what his wealth has created.

"This is a very proud and happy day for my family and for me," he began in his simple speech. "I can tell you that my family and I shall remember this day when the Almighty made it possible for my family to present Camp Davidowitz to the Jewish community of Hazleton."

When he died, three years later, his wife, Rose, continued his civic and synagogue work. Until her death, fourteen years later, she served on the board of every Jewish committee in town. A picture of her in 1967, when she was honored by the Jewish community, shows her, a short and stocky woman in her mid-sixties, with dark hair, her face still unlined.

Rose's daughter Sophie was the second of the three girls, bright and attractive. A picture in her high-school yearbook shows her with shoulder-length dark hair and a radiant smile. With hindsight the radiance appears sadly naive, but at the time, her life seemed full of promise. She was the girl who had everything—wealth, a loving family, close friends. Her large house on Aspen Street, in the best section of town, was the meeting place for her girlfriends, and the poorer Jewish boys from the outlying coal towns who came to Hazleton to meet Jewish girls considered it a treat to visit the Davidowitz house to pick up their dates.

After being graduated from high school, in September ‚1943, Sophie left Hazleton for Philadelphia, where she entered Temple University. She was twenty-one in 1947, with a degree in liberal arts, when she met Charles Friedgood, then a surgical resident at the University of Pennsylvania Hospital under Isidor Ravdin. Within the first six years of her marriage she bore him six children. From all accounts she adored him, right until the moment she died.

/ ii

Friedgood and Sophie moved to Brooklyn in 1950, when he left Mount Sinai for Maimonides Hospital. Until a few years before, Maimonides had been two separate small and second-rate hospitals, in the middle-class and heavily Jewish Borough Park section of Brooklyn, which at that time was also the home of the largest group of Orthodox and Hasidic Jews in the world. During the postwar years the hospitals had gone through something of a revolution; they had combined into one institution, a full-time chief surgeon had been appointed, and a residency program begun. Years later those affiliated with the hospital at the time would refer grandiloquently to those years as Maimonides' "golden age."

The surgical program, which consisted of fewer than two dozen residents, was small and competitive. The residents worked long hours, and in the empty afternoons their wives met in the hospital cafeteria to exchange stories. Before long, when the wives assembled in the cafeteria or when the residents and their wives met at parties, the first thing they found themselves talking about was Charles Friedgood.

Like all the other residents, he was eligible for free samples from many baby-food and vitamin companies, among them the company that made Similac baby formula. Friedgood was so greedy, and wrote away for so many samples, that soon he had a surplus to pass out to all the other residents and to his surgical chief, a brilliant young Canadian, Dr. Charles Ripstein.

Nor were the free samples confined to baby formula. "He could get anything free," recalled Ripstein's wife, Barbara. "We never paid for a glass of milk." When the Ripsteins had a baby, strange, unexpected cartons began to appear. Milk, shoes, free diaper service for a month. "We had a little apartment," Barbara Ripstein remembered, "that was filled to the ceiling with all the stuff he provided."

Then there were the free drugs the pharmaceutical houses provided the residents. Friedgood had written to them claiming he needed the drugs for research. Instead he sold them to local druggists.

Friedgood was, however, engaged in some drug research. At the time, doctors were experimenting with a potential cure for kidney and urinary-tract infection, a drug called Furadantin, and Friedgood himself began investigating it. He wrote a paper on it for a medical journal, and as the drug became known he claimed to be its codiscoverer and referred to it around the hospital as "my drug." Soon he was writing and telephoning doctors all across the country, trying to persuade them to come to New York City, where he had arranged conferences to discuss Furadantin research. He would then rush out to the airport to meet them when they arrived, and chauffeur them about the city. "He would do anything, go anywhere, claim anything," one resident remembered years later. "We were all convinced he would end up either president of General Motors or in jail." Furadantin proved to be a disappointment as a wonder drug and soon passed into obscurity—but Charles Friedgood did not.

At Maimonides' traditional New Year's party that year,

held in the hospital auditorium, the other residents put on a series of skits called "The Bo' Park Follies" (the title reflected the neighboring Hasidic Jews' pronunciation of "Borough Park"). The skits were a parody of hospital life, and woven through them was a character who appeared onstage to the accompaniment of gales of laughter from the audience. The character was dressed in doctor's whites, a stethoscope protruding from his pocket. He was fawning, smiling, interrupting each actor on the stage by shaking hands and insisting on introducing himself. "Hello, how are you feeling? Do you need a doctor? Do you need a surgeon? Do you want an operation? I'm Dr. Charles Friedgood."

/ iii

Then there was Friedgood's relationship with Sophie—the envy of the other residents' wives because of Friedgood's apparent successes. Kind, pretty, though on the heavy side now, Sophie seemed perpetually pregnant. "When she was pregnant for the second or third time," recalled one of the wives years later, "I told her how sorry I was. 'Oh, no,' she answered, 'I'm thrilled. Charlie wants a big family. He's very religious. It's part of the Jewish tradition.' "

There is a picture of Sophie in those early years of her marriage. In it she is holding her first child, David, who with his curly blond hair resembles his father. In the picture she is wearing, in the style of the 1950s, a long checkered dress, her dark hair swept back and over her shoulders. As the child, swaddled in a snowsuit, laughs and faces the camera, Sophie, oblivious of the camera, is smiling adoringly down at her baby.

To the other wives at the hospital, Sophie talked endlessly about her husband, his career, and her children. "She had warmth, affection," one of them recalled. "She cared for the next person. And she believed in Charlie." Yet to those wives who at first had envied her there was something sad, almost pathetic about her. To them it became apparent she knew little about her husband. Behind her back they laughed at her. Though she never then would have understood why, behind her back they called her "poor Sophie."

Once she gave a birthday party for little David. She ordered a cake from the local bakery and invited a number of other residents and their wives who also had children. Soon it was time for the child's birthday cake, and Friedgood said he would go to the bakery to pick it up. They all waited for him. They waited the entire afternoon, but he never returned.

Then there was the New Year's party given by one of the residents. Sophie arrived by herself just before ten o'clock. "Charlie will be here in a little while," she told everyone. When he did not appear, Sophie assured everybody he was at the hospital, obviously tied up with an emergency case. Finally, past midnight, when he still hadn't appeared, one of the residents called the hospital. There was no Charlie. He hadn't been at the hospital all night.

/ iv

To his fellow residents the most galling aspect about Charlie Friedgood was his relationship with the Hasidic Jews, who appeared regularly at the hospital's free surgical clinic. Poor, ignorant of all but religious concerns, the Hasidim strictly observed Orthodox Jewish law and, living in small enclaves, insulated themselves from the outside world to keep intact all the customs of their movement, which had been founded in eighteenth-century Eastern Europe.

As they had two hundred years before, the Hasidim encouraged large families. Their appearance—the men in full beards and *payess*, or long sideburns; the women with shaved heads and *sheitels*, or wigs—was the same as it had been across twenty decades. To them every act, however trivial it might seem to an outsider, was invested with mystical significance.

Their clothing was white and black, colors that symbolized compassion and mercy. They shunned anything in red because it represented blood and impurity. They would not wear ties and kept their shoes unlaced to avoid making knots on their bodies. They insisted on buttoning their coats from right—the symbol of mercy and love—to left—the symbol of justice and strength—so that mercy would dominate their lives. Central to their lives was their total dependence on the *tzaddikim,* or spiritual leaders, who guided and advised the Hasidim on every aspect of their lives, and whose dynastic names derived from the towns of their Eastern European ancestors—Lubavitch, Satmar, Belz, Bobov, Vishnitz, Ger, and Skvera.

How Charlie Friedgood's relationship with the Hasidim began none of the other residents seemed to know. Whereas they themselves were disdainful of, or embarrassed by, the Hasidim, Friedgood seemed to be forever smiling at them. He was especially ingratiating to one of their rabbis, a man with a florid complexion and flowing red beard, who appeared at the clinic as their official medical adviser and whom the other residents condescendingly referred to as "Red Beard." He was the Grand Rabbi.

Just what Charlie Friedgood saw in the Hasidim the other residents did not understand. He was not religious. He knew virtually no Hebrew. Yet as he had once charmed an audience in Detroit with an impassioned speech about Palestine, now he took to wearing a *yarmulke* on his head and speaking in Yiddish when he was covering the clinic. What was even more surprising—which even those residents who despised him had to admit—was that with these poor, ignorant Hasidim, Charlie Friedgood was always patient and kind. He never stopped smiling. He never lost his temper. He seemed actually to enjoy sitting and listening to them for hours.

The Hasidim were in awe of him. To them he was a healer with mystical qualities, not unlike their *tzaddikim.*

When he operated, they said he was *gebencht,* or blessed. Those who spoke English said he had "golden hands."

Soon, whenever a Hasid came to the clinic, he would ask to see Dr. Friedgood. Yet, devoted as he appeared to be, Friedgood never hesitated to charge them up to a hundred dollars for the surgery he performed, although hospital regulations specified that all surgery at the clinic was free. Once, a resident recalled, Friedgood operated on a woman and charged her seventy-five dollars. "She was so grateful to him. And he shouldn't have charged her a dime." In time, the hospital's chief of surgery, the brilliant young Canadian, Ripstein, learned Friedgood was charging patients and—though he could have dismissed him for this infraction, which was the height of immorality and the antithesis of medical ethics—he only ordered him to stop. Officially Friedgood stopped. Unofficially he continued.

When he was asked about these practices, Friedgood would smile and shrug. "If I didn't charge them, they would have been insulted. The Bible says: 'Anything that is free is worth nothing.' "

/ v

What most disturbed the other residents was Friedgood's surgery. Here the stories were no longer amusing, but frightening. Among themselves the residents now whispered the word that had been used to describe him in high school and college: amoral.

Years later a surgeon who had trained Friedgood explained that sometimes after a surgeon begins an operation, he is forced to back out of it because he discovers the surgery simply cannot be done. "The family may be upset," he explained, "but the surgeon must admit to them that he has failed. This was something Charlie could not do."

At first at Maimonides there were only hints, rumors

from residents who had scrubbed with him. There had been a "blue baby" who had been brought to Friedgood with a heart abnormality that caused an oxygen deficiency in the baby's blood. Friedgood performed surgery to correct the abnormality and charged the parents for it, but the baby did not improve. Baffled, the parents brought the baby to another surgeon, who discovered that only an incision had been made. No operation had been performed.

Yet the case was never investigated by the hospital staff. "Who would you tell?" asked a resident years later. "We were taught then never to testify against another doctor because you might be next. None of us would take the first step that might ruin Friedgood's career—or our own.

"We just didn't know what to do. It wasn't our responsibility. It was the surgical chief's. It was Ripstein's."

And Friedgood appeared to be close to Ripstein. The brilliant young Canadian—at the time of his appointment to Maimonides, it was said, he was already a member of the prestigious Royal College of Surgeons—was barely out of his own residency and not much older than the men he was training. And in the short time he had been at Maimonides he had remarkably upgraded the surgical program—putting an end to the practice of fee-splitting, and suspending the operating-room privileges of general practitioners.

Exactly what Friedgood's relationship with Ripstein was is unclear. But, as he did with many other eminent surgeons, Friedgood seemed to exert a hypnotic hold over him. Though Ripstein could have dismissed him from the clinic for charging fees, he had only reprimanded him. Then Ripstein discovered that Friedgood was telling the Hasidic patients at the clinic that Friedgood had trained Ripstein and that Ripstein was his assistant. Ripstein became incensed. At his wife's urging, he decided to confront Friedgood.

The night before he was to see Friedgood, she primed him on what he should say. The following afternoon, when

Ripstein went to the hospital, her relatives, who lived nearby, came to the house to await news.

"Well?" they demanded when Ripstein returned that evening. "What happened? What did you say to him? What did you do?"

Ripstein sadly shook his head. "What did I do?" he said. "I apologized."

So Friedgood was permitted to stay on.

Then, after his fourth year of residency, Friedgood decided to leave Maimonides and go into private practice. But— despite the rumors about him, despite Ripstein's own problems with him—to everyone's astonishment, Ripstein created a position for Friedgood as his special assistant.

Afterward Ripstein would refuse to discuss Friedgood, hanging up the telephone when his name was mentioned. "Ethics," his wife would say, trying to explain her husband's actions. "Principles. My husband has very strong principles." And, in what was clearly closer to her desire than to reality, she would blurt out, "I *think* my husband fired him."

6

IN FACT, RIPSTEIN COULD NEVER BRING HIMSELF TO fire Friedgood. The following year, Ripstein left Maimonides to become the first chief of surgery at the Albert Einstein College of Medicine. He was succeeded by Alfred Hurwitz, a tall, aloof New Englander who was regarded by his colleagues as a no-nonsense administrator and, as one of them put it, "a man with guts." One of the first things Hurwitz did at Maimonides was dismiss Charles Friedgood.

Among the Hasidim there was an outcry. Though Hurwitz was a Jew, there were whispers all through Borough Park that he was an anti-Semite. Finally the Grand Rabbi went to see Hurwitz to intercede for Friedgood. "Dr. Friedgood has done so much good in the Jewish community," the rabbi began.

But Hurwitz cut him off. "Don't speak to me of Friedgood," he shouted at the rabbi. "I don't want to hear anything more about him."

"I believe in calling a spade a spade," Hurwitz remembered twenty-five years later. "I believe there are people we must weed out. Friedgood was something I felt I had inherited. I felt I just had to do it."

Twenty-five years later Hurwitz could not remember exactly what had precipitated his dismissal of Friedgood. But twenty-five years later he vividly remembers his last meeting with him. "I'll kill you," Friedgood shouted at him after Hurwitz told him he was fired. "I'll get you and pay you back. I'll get you if it's the last thing I ever do."

Yet Friedgood never asked for a hearing at the hospital, to which he was entitled. Hurwitz never saw him again.

Maimonides was not required to notify any medical body of Friedgood's dismissal. Apparently no written record was made of the reasons. A dismissal of any kind would not help a hospital trying to upgrade itself. As the hospital's administrator, William Horner, put it, "We don't withhold such information. But we don't notify other hospitals, either."

Twenty-five years later Maimonides would even claim it had no record of the years Friedgood worked there; Horner said the records had been destroyed in a fire. "It's a litigious community," Maimonides' counsel, Daniel Ginsberg, explained. "There is always the fear of a malpractice suit."

And so Charles Friedgood was able to continue to practice.

Afterward, when asked about his dismissal from Maimonides, Friedgood would shake his head, smile, shrug. "I was dismissed because of personal jealousies, because I was so close to Ripstein. When he left, so did I."

And despite his dismissal, Friedgood continued to list himself year after year in the *Directory of Medical Specialists* as "full-time associate in surgery 1952–[through present] Maimonides Hospital, Brooklyn."

/ ii

From Maimonides, Friedgood returned to Philadelphia. He did not return to Ravdin or the University of Pennsylvania Hospital. Instead he applied to a residency program in cardiovascular surgery at Hahnemann Medical School. Hahnemann's cardiovascular department was headed by a brilliant and maverick surgeon, a pioneer in open-heart surgery in the days before the invention of the heart-and-lung machine, which enables blood to bypass the heart during an operation.

Conventional medical terminology, this surgeon said, likened the heart's mitral valve—through which oxygenated blood passes from one chamber of the heart to another—to a human mouth. "But I saw it more as a female girdle, which I could pull and stretch with my fingers." Operating in the dark, pulling and tugging at the mitral valve, relying on his sense of touch—which he had perfected as an amateur photographer in his darkroom—he began performing crude open-heart surgery.

But because the surgeon's methods were new and unconventional, and because he insisted on operating when chances of success were minimal—his first nine patients died on the operating table, and only the tenth survived—his work was never truly honored by the American College of Surgeons. To the surgical establishment he was a pariah.

Like Friedgood, the surgeon had studied under Ravdin, who had also been skeptical of his approach. But Ravdin was still a potent name to him, and when Friedgood said that he, too, had worked with Ravdin, the surgeon accepted him into his program. But he never called Ravdin to inquire about Friedgood. He relied only on Friedgood's word.

Friedgood spent a year under him in Philadelphia. "What I remember most about Charlie were his hands," the surgeon recalled. "Beautiful, beautiful hands. Technically he was a fine surgeon, but—" The surgeon paused. "There was always something wrong."

Exactly what disturbed him the surgeon had difficulty explaining. It was, he remembered, more a *feeling* than anything he could prove. "If Charlie failed to do something, he was likely to weasel out of it by a bold statement. Frequently I would discover a grave discrepancy between what he said he had done and what he actually had done." Once, he recalled, he told Friedgood to tap a patient's chest. Later Friedgood told the surgeon he had successfully extracted 1,500 cc's of fluid from the patient. But the attending nurse informed the surgeon that the patient had resisted and that Friedgood had been unable to tap his chest.

The surgeon realized that whenever Friedgood told him anything, he had to check it out himself. And whenever Friedgood was on call at the hospital, he took care that a second surgeon was also on the floor.

Still, as the surgeon explained, "Charlie was so likable." When Friedgood returned to New York, they parted friends. Through the years they continued to see each other, Friedgood always calling his old teacher "Chief." When Friedgood's third daughter, Beth, was born (the Hebrew diminutive of her name, Bela, happened to resemble the surgeon's last name), he told the surgeon he had named her after him.

Later, when the surgeon moved to New York, Friedgood recommended patients to him. Periodically he would come to the surgeon and ask for his help as he ran into trouble at the hospitals that later employed him. And during the bad years, when Friedgood's hospitals—the small, poorer ones— were being closed down one by one, he asked the surgeon whether he might become his associate.

/ iii

After his year at Hahnemann, Friedgood returned to Brooklyn. He joined the staff of Beth El (now Brookdale) Hospital, another small hospital that, like Maimonides, was trying to upgrade itself. Recently the hospital had hired as its chief surgeon Friedgood's former patron Harold Neuhof, by then retired from Mount Sinai. Under him, in September 1955, Friedgood joined the staff as a "provisional assistant in cardiovascular surgery."

Yet in January 1957, just over a year after his appointment, Friedgood was dismissed from Beth El. Again like Maimonides, the hospital gave no written reasons for his dismissal. "The committee on reappointments has failed to take affirmative action on your reappointment," read the vaguely worded letter telling him that he would not be rehired.

"He pulled a couple of dishonest things," explained a surgeon who had trained at Maimonides with Friedgood and was on the staff of Beth El at the time of Friedgood's appointment. "He would pass by a room where there were two or three patients. The next thing you'd know, their regular doctors had been discharged and Friedgood was their new doctor. He once visited another doctor's patient in the morning—she had an intestinal obstruction. In the afternoon he was preparing to operate on her. But he wasn't her doctor—someone else was. Of course you couldn't put that in the record."

So again Friedgood was able to continue.

Friedgood had the same answer to questions about his dismissal from Beth El as he had about his firing from Maimonides: "Politics. They were jealous because I was close to Neuhof. When he left, so did I." But in his surgeon's directory, he would make no mention of his ever having worked at Beth El.

/ iv

He next joined the staff of the Veterans Administration Hospital in Brooklyn as a thoracic surgeon, but remained only a year. Again the reasons for his leaving are not clear. In fact the VA Hospital says it has no record of Friedgood's ever having practiced there.

He then joined the staff of the Downstate Medical Center in Brooklyn as an assistant professor of general surgery. Two years later, in 1957, he was not rehired "due to changes in the curriculum." Again no record was made of the reasons for his dismissal. And in the medical directory he continued to list himself as an "assistant professor of surgery 1952–[through present]."

In the late 1950s he applied to Long Island Jewish Hospital. The head of surgery, who had known him from the VA Hospital, turned him down. "He'd get into this hospital over my dead body," he explained. But the surgeon never committed to writing just what his reasons were. Again Friedgood was able to continue.

/ v

Dismissed from the first rank of hospitals, Friedgood joined the second-rank ones. In 1960 he was one of the founders of Interboro Hospital, an osteopathic clinic at the edge of Brooklyn's Brownsville section, on Linden Boulevard, not far from Kennedy Airport. Once the home of a poor but thriving Jewish community, the area had lost its younger and more successful residents, many of whom had moved east to the suburbs in Long Island, and who had been replaced by blacks and Puerto Ricans.

For Friedgood, Interboro Hospital was a business as well as a medical venture. He was one of forty-two doctors who became partners in the hospital. He also became a member of the corporation that owned the hospital buildings and the land, which stretched for three or four blocks along Linden Boulevard, the main thoroughfare of the neighborhood. But later, as the hospital improved, he was dismissed from there as well. Still, with his following among the Hasidim, his practice throve. In the mid-1950s he opened an office in Brooklyn's Crown Heights section, where the Hasidic Lubavitcher sect was centered. The neighborhood was a middle-class one, not unlike the old neighborhood on Detroit's west side where he had grown up. The mansions that bordered tree-lined Eastern Parkway might as well have been on Boston or Chicago Boulevard, where Detroit's richest Jews lived. And the poorer thoroughfares that ran into Eastern Parkway, like Rogers and Nostrand avenues, could have been copies of LaSalle Boulevard, where he had lived as a boy.

Friedgood's office at 277 Eastern Parkway was just two bare, unpainted rooms. No pictures on the walls, no plants, no decorations—simply an examination room and a waiting room with plastic and wooden folding chairs. Like his Hasidic patients, Friedgood appeared to have rejected the trappings of worldly success. No longer, as in the flush of his first marriage, did he wear new gabardine suits, silk ties, or expensive shoes. In fact he rarely wore a doctor's white coat. His clothes were old and worn. He did not care that his jacket never matched his pants. His hair was uncombed, his shoes scruffy and unshined. The only luxury he allowed himself was a new Cadillac he rented each year. Despite its bare and shabby appearance, his office was always filled with patients, and from eight in the morning until five in the evening Friedgood was either there or in Interboro Hospital's operating room; often he worked late into the evening, not leaving his office until after midnight.

He worked six days a week. He treated forty to fifty patients a day. He did twenty to twenty-five operations a week—on hearts, hernias, gallbladders, rectums, broken bones, stomachs, lungs, and intestines. Ignorant, uneducated, and superstitious, his patients never worried that many of these operations were outside his field of expertise; nor did they wonder why he sometimes operated on a patient ten, fifteen, or twenty times, then encouraged him to bring his family to be operated on as well.

Ninety-five percent of his patients were on Medicare or Medicaid. Thus, they rarely paid him directly themselves. Ignorant and uneducated as they were, they believed he was operating on them for free.

Soon Friedgood was known among the Hasidim from

Crown Heights to Borough Park to Williamsburg. Sometimes the rabbis themselves came to him for surgery. Once an important *tzaddik* cut his hand deeply with steel wool. Friedgood operated on him in his office with no anesthetic. Afterward the rabbi told his followers, "He saved my hand."

And he did more than surgery. There were favors the rabbis asked of him. Often people needed a doctor to fill out certain forms—many of the rabbis' followers were refugees from concentration camps and qualified for reparations from the German government for medical disabilities. All that was needed was a letter from a doctor certifying the disability. Whenever a rabbi came with a letter to Dr. Friedgood, he could depend on the doctor's signing it.

As they had done among the residents at Maimonides Hospital, the stories about him became legion among the Hasidim. There was the tale of the ninety-year-old Lubavitcher rabbi, spiritual leader of thousands, who had come to Friedgood with advanced cancer of the colon. Doctors had refused to operate on him because of his age. But Friedgood removed the cancer, then removed one hundred stones from his urinary bladder. Ten days later the old man walked out of the hospital.

Then there was the story of a man Friedgood had cured of leprosy after other doctors had been unable to—he had even restored the man's face to its former shape. And it was said that Friedgood had cured the pope of hiccups. The Hasidim would point to the Latin words on a plaque on Friedgood's wall. It was a message of thanks, they said, signed by the pontiff himself.

Soon his office began to resemble a neighborhood political clubhouse. While he treated his patients, friends, business associates, and passersby in their long black coats and beards wandered in and out. A few years later, in the early 1960s, when his parents moved to New York, they rented an apartment just ten minutes from his office and visited him there each day. Though he was retired now, his father, Ichy, had not finished buying and selling. One day a week he would drive across the Brooklyn Bridge to Manhattan and uptown to the Garment Center. From jobbers there he would buy leftover lots—jackets, shirts, ties, pairs of socks—put them in his car, drive back across the bridge to his son's office, then sell them to patients in the waiting room for a quarter or fifty cents.

Meanwhile his mother, Chafke, would bring in fresh fruit and vegetables for her son. Sometimes she would help answer his telephone. "Hello. You want to speak to the doctor? What's the matter with you?" she would say to the caller, then proceed to give a diagnosis herself. Sometimes when he treated patients she would sit, silent and smiling, in the rear of his office, proudly watching her son.

/ vi

Friedgood kept no formal office records. Nor did he employ a bookkeeper or even a nurse. Instead his office was staffed by former female patients he had operated on who afterward offered to work for him on a part-time basis, and whom he paid off the books. To these women Friedgood displayed what appeared to be great kindness. One of them, nicknamed Blackie, was a grandmother in her sixties, the wife of a rabbi who came from a family of rabbis. She had first met Friedgood in 1955 when her mother was dying of stomach cancer. "He came to her home in the middle of the night," Blackie recalled. "What would you like?" she remembered his saying to the old lady. "A cup of coffee? Some tea?"

He had then ordered Blackie's sister to make the old lady a cup of coffee. Standing at the patient's bedside, he gave it to her himself. There was nothing he could do, he told them; the cancer had spread. Still, he appeared at the house all the time, at all hours of the day and night, to look at the old lady and to give her injections to ease her pain.

At the same time, Blackie's mother-in-law also developed cancer, and Friedgood operated on her. "He did not save her life," said Blackie. "But he told my sister-in-law she would live about a year, without pain, and then die peacefully. And she did, just as he said she would."

When, the following year, Blackie began suffering from ulcers, she also went to Dr. Friedgood. Friedgood operated. Late at night, following the operation, when she was half asleep, dozing, filled with painkillers and medication, he appeared at her bedside.

"Open your eyes," she heard him saying to her. "Do you know who I am?"

"Yes," she answered.

"Go back to sleep," he commanded her.

"Would any other doctor have come to see me in the middle of the night?" she says now. "Would any other doctor have done that?"

Over the years, Friedgood operated on Blackie for a gallbladder condition, for hemorrhoids, and for cancer. He performed a hysterectomy on her. He also operated on her sister's hernia and varicose veins; on both her brothers; on her sister-in-law; and on assorted cousins.

It was the same with Friedgood's second receptionist. Her name was Suzie Bren, and she was an attractive, though overweight, woman in her thirties whose husband had died of a stroke and left her with four small children. As he had done with Blackie, Friedgood displayed great concern for Suzie Bren. She would be astonished, and flattered, that he would sit with her for hours, it seemed, after his patients had gone, teaching her medical terminology.

He would also operate on her, as he had on Blackie. Years later Suzie Bren would talk about the thyroid operation Friedgood performed that she was convinced had saved her life. One summer she had worked as a hostess in a Catskills resort so that her children could attend its day camp for free.

One morning she felt a lump in her throat. She rushed to New York to see Friedgood.

"He felt the lump and immediately took me across the street to Interboro Hospital for a thyroid scan. After the scan he put me right into the hospital. Because I was so nervous he stayed with me until I got settled in bed. I was operated on the next day. The morning of my operation he visited me. 'Don't be afraid. Don't be afraid,' he kept telling me.

"Then, after the operation, he came into the recovery room. I was black and blue from the surgery and they wouldn't even let me look in the mirror. But Dr. Friedgood made me talk. He visited me four and five times a day. He even read the newspapers and magazines to me."

Years later, after he had been imprisoned and she had found work as a legal secretary, Suzie Bren often pointed to her scar, which was barely visible where it ran across her throat. "You see," she would tell people, "you can hardly see it. That's how good he was."

He displayed a similar concern for Suzie Bren's younger cousin. Like Suzie Bren, she was extremely overweight; she was also on the verge of dropping out of high school. Often as Friedgood made his rounds at the hospitals he would take the girl with him; he would talk to her while he sutured his patients, encouraging her to remain in school so someday she might become a nurse. Years later, after the trial, he would write Suzie long, chatty letters from Greenhaven Prison ("Greetings from Greenhaven—which is neither green nor a haven") telling her of the work he was doing at the prison hospital, asking for news about herself and her cousin, who had completed high school and had entered nursing school.

And as he had operated on Suzie Bren, he also operated on her cousin. When she was seventeen years old, she asked him to perform an operation—known as an intestinal bypass—that he had begun doing experimentally on his patients who wished to lose weight. At first, Suzie Bren remembered,

Friedgood had objected, saying that the operation—which permits food to pass almost directly from the stomach to the large intestine, bypassing the small intestine and thereby avoiding being absorbed by the body—is fraught with risk. There can be severe consequences, from gallstones to kidney stones to urinary infections to liver failure, and even—in one case out of fifteen—death. And patients often put back the weight they lose. The operation is rarely performed today, and most reputable surgeons have given up on it because it just does not work.

Yet the girl insisted, and finally Friedgood consented. But the operation wasn't successful. Besides regaining all the weight, the girl began suffering such severe aftereffects from the surgery that for years she was in and out of hospitals. Suzie Bren never forgave herself for having brought her cousin to Friedgood. Though she had no hesitation in talking about the thyroid operation he had so expertly performed on her, the subject of her cousin was so painful that for years she could not bring herself to speak of it. And yet she never blamed Friedgood for the failure of the operation.

/ vii

But unknown to Blackie, unknown to Suzie Bren, unknown to his Hasidic patients and their rabbis, there was another side to Charles Friedgood. True, he appeared to care nothing for the finery money could buy and practiced among the poor in deteriorating neighborhoods. Yet at the same time, Charlie Friedgood, as one of his daughters later told a district attorney, "was obsessed with money."

With the money he earned from his practice, with his wife's money, which had been settled on her by her family, even with the money from Sophie's family left in trust for his children, he began investing with unlikely partners in questionable business deals: in nursing homes; in land in upstate

Monticello, where Orthodox Jews lived; in Coney Island's amusement parks' Cyclone ride; and in a Holiday Inn franchise near Kennedy Airport.

And late at night, long after Blackie and Suzie Bren had left, after his last scheduled patient had gone, he performed other operations.

In early 1964 a woman in her early twenties named Evelyn Handelman appeared in Friedgood's office. She had been recommended by one of Friedgood's business partners, a stockbroker named Jerry Gottlieb.

Evelyn Handelman had been recommended to Dr. Charles Friedgood because she was four months pregnant and needed an abortion. Because in 1964 abortions were illegal, Friedgood could, and did, command a high price to perform them—a thousand dollars.

The following week, in his office, Friedgood performed an abortion on Evelyn Handelman. But her bleeding, which was supposed to stop in a few days, worsened instead. Two days later she was hemorrhaging so severely that she was rushed to a hospital with what a doctor there diagnosed as "a badly executed and almost fatal abortion."

The hospital notified the police. In July 1964 police obtained a wiretap order signed by State Supreme Court Justice Francis X. Conlon, and later extended by Judge Mitchell Schweitzer, for Friedgood's office telephone. By the fall there was evidence that Friedgood had done eight abortions—including Evelyn Handelman's—dating back to 1961. In December 1964 Friedgood and Gottlieb were indicted on eight counts of abortion and manslaughter of an infant. Preliminary hearings were set for April.

By then Evelyn Handelman had married and moved upstate. After the indictments were handed down, she pleaded with the Brooklyn district attorney, Aaron Koota, not to use her as a witness. Her husband, she told Koota, had believed she was a virgin when she married him. "I will testify if you force me to," she said to him, "but then I will kill myself because my whole life will be ruined."

Aaron Koota, who was later to become a New York State Supreme Court justice, never forgot Evelyn Handelman. "I remember the case very well," he said afterward. "I remember it so well because the woman was not hysterical when she said she would kill herself. She was very calm and I believed her."

Koota was not an unfeeling man. He discussed Evelyn Handelman with his associates. They had, they felt, witnesses from the seven other cases turned up by the wiretaps. Believing the testimony from them would be sufficient, they agreed that Evelyn Handelman need not testify.

In the meantime, Friedgood had hired perhaps the best-known criminal-law firm in Brooklyn—Kleinman, Gold and Landsman—to defend him. William Kleinman, the founder, was both a flamboyant and a controversial figure, who seemed, as *The New York Times* put it in his obituary a few years later, "to have appeared in every celebrated case in the New York courts."

He had begun his career as an assistant district attorney more than thirty years before in Brooklyn, where he became the subject of a *cause célèbre* when he was accused of accepting a bribe for protecting a convicted murderer. At his trial he defended himself, "summoning in his own behalf," as an account at the time put it, "all the skill and eloquence he used in years past to convict others." His eloquence was apparently persuasive. He was acquitted, though he was forced to resign from the DA's staff.

He then went into private practice, defending through the years an assortment of criminals from Russian spies to Louis "Lepke" Buchalter of Murder Inc. During World War II he served as a colonel in an infantry division and as the years passed he came to enjoy being referred to by his old army rank. As "the Colonel" grew older he took to walking with a cane, which became his trademark around the city's courtrooms. Fittingly, when he died in 1969, he was stricken in a federal courtroom—where he was defending a local Teamster official accused of a kickback scheme.

By 1964, when Friedgood came to him, he had taken in his son-in-law as a partner, together with a bright, ambitious young fellow named Eugene Gold, who four years later, when Aaron Koota was elevated to the bench, succeeded him as Brooklyn DA. Throughout the 1960s, as Kleinman's associate, Gold had specialized in wiretapping cases. Years later he would boast he had pioneered in making a new wiretap law. It seemed only natural that he be given the Friedgood case.

What happened next is not easy to establish, for here the story grows murky; and the court records that would make the case clear are now either lost, destroyed, or hidden in the Brooklyn district attorney's office, which is still occupied by Kleinman's former partner, Eugene Gold. But in March 1965 a hearing was held in Brooklyn before State Supreme Court Justice Dominic Rinaldi. Two days later Rinaldi ruled that "any and all leads and clues or any information directly or indirectly obtained as a result of the telephone wiretapping" was illegal. Without Evelyn Handelman to testify, Friedgood was a free man.

Little notice was taken of the case by the newspapers or by anyone else. A three-paragraph story that appeared in the New York *Daily News* was the only reference in the newspapers. The last paragraph quoted one of Friedgood's attorneys, who said that Friedgood had won many honors in the medical profession.

Nor was an investigation begun or any action taken against Friedgood by the medical profession. Once again he was allowed to continue.

Part II

THE FAMILY

7

OF THE CHILDREN, IT WAS THE DAUGHTERS WHO became players in the family tragedy. The boys, their two brothers, seem not to have been strong enough to assume a role. Pushed to become physicians like their father, neither did. Instead, David, the smiling eldest child, whom as a baby Sophie so adored, fled to the Midwest, where he married and became an osteopath. After Sophie's death he named his first child after her. By then he had changed his own last name.

The younger son, Stephen, drifted in and out of schools and careers. He had no part in the drama that would make his family famous, and at its end, when his father's role was terrifyingly clear, simply could not accept it. "I don't know what to believe," the newspapers quoted him as saying at the end of the trial. "What would you believe if it were your father?"

At least in the early years the children were spared the anguish that later engulfed them. Looking back on it all through their descriptions of their childhood—their relationship with their mother and father, the religious school, summer camp, and family vacations—one is struck by how happy they all seemed.

They lived in an old firehouse near Maimonides Hospital that had been converted into a tiny two-floor private house, in a section where on warm nights neighbors gossiped on their front porches and children played hide-and-seek by climbing through their front windows. With Friedgood always away treating patients at the hospital or at his office on Eastern Parkway, the children's education was left to Sophie. As she herself had done, she wanted her children to learn Yiddish and Hebrew. The school she selected was the Yeshiva of Flatbush, a private religious school. Their tuition was paid by her parents, the Davidowitzes.

In the morning, before the children left for school, Sophie would line the little girls up and, one by one, would brush their hair into the braids they all wore. Then she sliced oranges and arranged them on the kitchen table for each of the children.

She had set up a "buddy system" for them. Each of the three older children was to take care of one of the younger ones: David, the eldest, was little Stephen's buddy; Beth and Esther, the two middle children, were paired; and Toba, the eldest girl, shy and heavyset, was given Dvorah, or Debbie, the youngest daughter, who was small and plump, with a mischievous smile. Each morning Sophie would wave to them from her window as they left for school, three pairs of children holding hands as they walked together to the school bus.

Sophie also insisted the family observe *Shabbos*. Every Friday night she would put a kerchief on her head and welcome the Sabbath, lighting the candles as the children recited the prayer with her. In their *Shabbos* ceremony, the youngest daughter, Debbie, would say the blessing every Friday over the wine. The younger son, Stephen, would say the blessing over the bread. Then their father said, *"Baruch atah, Adonoi"* ("Blessed art thou, our God"), and they would all laugh when, because he did not know the Hebrew words, he would add in English, "May you do well in school!" or "May you do well on your tests!"

On the Jewish High Holidays Sophie would lead them all to synagogue. She would dress the little girls alike, in gray-and-white dresses with red berets and white gloves. As they walked together, the neighbors would stare and smile at them—a husband, wife, and six small children, such a lovely-looking family.

As the last of her children started classes, Sophie herself began thinking of returning to school. In college she had been a fine student, interested in science. But there was already a scientist in the family. She decided to enter Brooklyn Law School. During the day, with the children at school, she attended classes. In the evening, as the children sat around the dining table doing their homework, Sophie sat with them, checking their homework and doing her own at the same time.

Summers the children all attended camp in upstate New York, their tuition again paid by Sophie's parents. After camp they all drove out to Montauk Point, at the tip of Long Island, and rented a bungalow. At night they turned off all the lights, made a fire, and listened to their mother tell ghost stories.

During the winter holidays they would spend a week at a small hotel called Young's Gap in the Catskills at Monticello, New York. For New Year's Eve there was a party, with costumes. During the week Sophie took pictures of the children skiing, and their father took pictures of Sophie ice-skating.

They traveled everywhere in an old station wagon. David, the eldest, and little Debbie sat in the back, in the third seat. Stephen sat in the gap between the back and middle seats. Toba sat in the middle seat, between her two younger sisters: Beth, who was dark and quiet, and Esther, who was lively, blond, and fair-skinned like her grandmother Chafke, her father's mother.

Their parents sat in front, and wherever they traveled, their father always drove. Sophie sat next to him holding a big bag filled with oranges and sandwiches that she would pass out to the children. Driving through the mountains or out to the end of Long Island, they all sang songs. Their father sang his old college songs from the University of Michigan—"Hail to the victors valiant/ Hail to the conquering heroes"—and their mother sang songs from her college days at Temple. Together they joined in songs that they had known growing up in the 1930s and 1940s, "My Blue Heaven" or "Look for the Silver Lining." Each had a favorite tune—their father's was the old setting of Kipling's poem "On the Road to Mandalay"; their mother's was a Yiddish song she had learned as a girl, "Bim-bom."

And the whole family sang "The Seven of Us and You." It went:

> Where are we going, what are we doing?
> What are we going to do?
> We're on our way to somewhere.
> The seven of us and you.

/ ii

Then their world crumbled. "It was early in the morning and we were getting ready for school," Debbie remembered. "I was six. I remember hearing my mother screaming, 'Charles! Charles!' and my father racing up the stairs three at a time."

The children followed him to the bedroom door and looked inside. Sophie was sitting up in the bed crying. Their father lifted her up and tried to get her to stand. But she crumpled onto the floor.

She had, at age thirty-three, suffered a paralyzing stroke. Her mother, Rose Davidowitz, came up from Hazleton to help care for her in the hospital. Ichy and Chafke arrived from Detroit to stay with the children until she recovered. Three months later Sophie was brought home.

To the children she tried to act as though she were not sick. Her bed was placed in the middle of the living room and she tried to appear as though there were nothing the matter with her. A few months later she was able to move to a wheelchair and to the children she made it sound like wonderful news.

Sophie made an almost complete recovery. Only four toes on one foot remained paralyzed, causing a barely noticeable limp. Yet the stroke was to change her in ways none of them could have foreseen. She appeared bitter about it, cheated, the children sensed. At first she couldn't run. She couldn't dance. And she could not return to law school. Years later she would tell her daughters in a voice they had never heard before, "I came face-to-face with death. I could have succumbed. But I fought back for us. I had six children to raise."

To the children she now seemed a different person. She insisted they each must learn to play the piano. At summer camp they had to learn to swim. She demanded they earn all A's at school.

Now each daughter had to take dancing lessons. Esther, the most vivacious of them all, the one with the most confidence, the only one who was not afraid of this new, determined person Sophie had become, liked to sing and was given singing lessons. "Anything we could take a lesson in," she said, "we had it."

Soon there were golf and tennis and horseback-riding lessons as well—for, three years after Sophie's stroke, with the neighborhood around them deteriorating, the mansions on Eastern Parkway becoming vacant, West Indians and Hasidim moving into them, the Friedgoods left their tiny row house and, like thousands of other Brooklyn families, moved east to Long Island. They moved to the exclusive North Shore village of Kensington, where they purchased a fourteen-room brick Colonial house with nine bedrooms, two staircases, an enclosed porch, and a small front lawn. Everything changed in Kensington, the children said afterward. It was in Kensington that their real troubles began.

8

TO PEOPLE DRIVING OUT FROM NEW YORK CITY ON
the asphalt slab of concrete known as the Long Island Expressway, Long Island appears as an endless row of tract homes,
parking lots, and shopping malls, sprung apparently full
grown from the developer's bulldozer. From the Midtown
Tunnel running east through Queens and Long Island's suburban Nassau and more rural Suffolk counties, the expressway
bisects the island's flat midsection, running past towns and villages whose names sound more mid-American than urban—
New Hyde Park, Plainview, Melville, Hicksville, Medford,
Ronkonkoma, Wading River. Even those villages one hundred
miles from Times Square, the developers have not spared.
Long Island is flat, development quick and cheap. The model
homes run right up to the expressway; model villages are displayed along the service roads; and south of the expressway
appear house after house, row after row, development after
seemingly endless development.

Yet there is another Long Island, one of grace, charm,
elegance, of woods, fields, and hills, which cannot be seen, or
even imagined, from the expressway. North of it, actually

north of the Northern State Parkway, which the expressway follows and which forms a barrier separating it from the rest of the Island, the North Shore hills appear, then slope gently down toward Long Island Sound. Because of its beauty and its proximity to New York City, Long Island's North Shore had long been a convenient retreat for "gentlemen" engaged in business in the city. By the turn of the century North Shore farmland had been purchased by the nation's aristocracy—the Vanderbilts, Roosevelts, Morgans, Whitneys, and Mellons. Baronial estates were constructed, with elaborate mansions, private chapels, reservoirs, stables, and golf courses. One after the other they appeared, until they formed an almost unbroken chain running from the city's limits, at the edge of the metropolitan borough of Queens, through the Great Neck peninsula just over the Nassau County line, and then east through the towns of Old Westbury and Oyster Bay into Suffolk County. This swath of the North Shore was known as the Gold Coast.

The Great Neck peninsula, where half a century later Charles Friedgood was to settle, was part of, though somehow different from, the rest of the Gold Coast. During the 1920s it had become the favorite of the literary and show-business set—"the Suburban Riviera," as it was termed by Gene Buck, who while living in Great Neck wrote nineteen *Follies* for Florenz Ziegfeld.

P. G. Wodehouse lived there, as did Eddie Cantor, Fanny Brice, Ring Lardner, Ed Wynn, Leslie Howard, Maurice Chevalier, Fredric March, the Marx Brothers, and Herbert Bayard Swope. F. Scott Fitzgerald moved to Great Neck with his wife, Zelda, before they left for the real Riviera—at the time, they were struggling, it was said, on thirty-five thousand dollars a year. It was in Great Neck that Fitzgerald wrote *The Great Gatsby,* with the model for Jay Gatsby's improbable mansion said to be the nearby Booth estate—"A factual imitation of one Hotel de Ville in Normandy, with a tower on one side, spanking new under a thin beard of raw ivy, and a marble swimming pool, and more than four acres of lawn and garden."

Kensington, the two-mile-square section of Great Neck into which Charles Friedgood was to move, had been one of the nation's earliest and most elegant developments. It was founded in 1909 by a banker named Charles E. Finlay and a developer named E. J. Rickert, and its owners offered plots starting at the then exorbitant price of fifteen thousand dollars. In the next few years the developers planted eleven and a half miles of hedges. They paved five miles of roadway and eleven miles of sidewalk. They planted fifteen parks of different geometrical shapes at the curved intersections of village streets. Behind the private houses they placed all utility poles, wires, and pipes. They built sewers, a private swimming pool, private tennis courts, and a private school, and hired a private police force.

Then they published a brochure.

"It is Friday afternoon and you've hurried to clear up your desk so you can enjoy to the full your weekend with the Joneses at Kensington," the brochure began. "Phoning your wife to meet you on the 4:58 train in the L.I. section of Pennsylvania Station, you leave your office downtown at 4:40 and take the elevated to the Thirty-third Street station. Upon entering the train you note that the cars are modern steel coaches, well lighted, well ventilated and with seats for everyone. A consultation of your watch as the train gets in motion shows that you are leaving on the minute of 4:58 and as your wife is busy gossiping with Mrs. Jones—you and Jones settle yourselves for a leisurely perusal of your papers."

As for Kensington itself: "You enter Kensington through an imposing gateway, like that of a private estate, and immediately find yourself in a veritable fairyland of natural beauty. The main drive through the property known as Beverly Road is lined on either side with lindens and elms thirty years old forming a continuous archway of green for nearly three quarters of a mile. The macadamized roads, flanked by grass borders, beautiful trees, cement walks and hedges are all kept beautifully trimmed and clean through the Association system of general maintenance."

Nearly fifty years were to pass from when that brochure was written until the day in 1963 when Charles Friedgood moved his family from Brooklyn to the fourteen-room brick Colonial house at 47 Beverly Road. Much about the North Shore, if not all of Long Island, had changed. The postwar population boom had begun. Families from Brooklyn and Queens were buying homes pell-mell in the middle of the Island, in Hicksville, East Meadow, West Hempstead, and Levittown. They were city workers, cops and sanitation men, men who worked in factories in Brooklyn and got up at four A.M. to buck the traffic on the expressway, then returned home after dark and saw their children only on weekends. In Brooklyn and Queens these men had lived in apartments and voted Democratic. Now, in a Levitt-built development home on an eighty-by-one-hundred plot, they were suddenly homeowners and voting Republican.

Jewish and Italian mostly, the wealthier of them had spilled over to the South Shore, near the ocean, to Massapequa, Oceanside, the Five Towns, and Atlantic Beach. By the 1960s, as barriers against them began to fall, they—those few with even more money—had migrated north, across the expressway and the Northern State Parkway, to the North Shore.

By then Great Neck had also changed. The show-biz literary set had long since moved on. Their estates had been sold off during the Depression. Later they were subdivided and developed into split-level homes and garden apartments. Instead of actors or literati, the people who lived in them now were wealthy professionals, doctors, lawyers, and businessmen. Most of them were Jewish, and nearly all of them were rich.

Kensington, too, had changed. The fifteen geometrically shaped parks had all been filled in with new homes, none of which could be touched for under $100,000. An apartment house had even been built on Middleneck Road, which ran through Great Neck's heart, at the entrance to the Kensington gate. Still, much of the village charm remained. The Kensington Village Association still made street repairs, cut the grass, plowed the streets, and cleared the snow. The private pool and private tennis courts were still there. And the six-man private police force, separate from the larger and better-disciplined Nassau County Police Department, still patrolled the streets, checking parking meters, responding to calls about suspected burglars—suspicious, as Charles Friedgood was to discover, of any movement that might disturb the calm of a suburban day.

/ ii

This was the world into which Charles Friedgood had moved his family, but it seemed that he himself was never there. Now he left the house each morning at seven-thirty, joining the flow of traffic on the Long Island Expressway to the city, but instead of driving into Manhattan, as did most commuters, at the edge of Queens he looped south onto the Cross-Island Parkway, then onto the Belt Parkway, which runs past Kennedy Airport, around the southern edge of Brooklyn. There, on Linden Boulevard, at the edge of Brownsville, where two-family homes gave way to vacant lots, sits Interboro Hospital, and it was here, with his poor patients, far from Kensington's spacious houses and tree-lined streets, that Charles Friedgood maintained his practice.

Yet it was not just his practice that kept him away from Kensington. There was also his mother, Chafke. Soon after they had moved to Kensington his father, Ichy, had died. Not invited by Sophie to move with them to Kensington, the old lady refused to return to her daughter in Detroit, where she had lived most of her life. Instead she insisted on remaining near her son.

Friedgood found her an apartment near Interboro in a neighborhood where pockets of elderly Jews hung on amid the *bodegas* and social clubs. Two mornings a week, he picked her up at her apartment and brought her to his office or deposited her at the hospital, where he got her a job of sorts, reading newspapers and magazines to infirm, elderly patients. Saturdays he would also drive in from Kensington and accompany the old lady to one of the small, decaying synagogues. Then the two of them would walk to one of the nearby kosher delicatessens and have lunch.

His business dealings also kept him away from home—most importantly, his investment in the Holiday Inn near Kennedy Airport, which he had gone into with a builder named Toby Miller. He and Miller had met through the stockbroker Jerry Gottlieb, the "steerer" in Friedgood's abortion cases.

A short, ruddy, athletic man with carefully maintained brown hair and a ready smile, Miller had been a semipro ballplayer before turning to business, and Holiday Inns. His philosophy—his view of business and of people—was crude and direct. As he put it later, after he and Friedgood had fallen out, "Sooner or later everything comes down to money."

Miller had purchased the land and the building for his first Holiday Inn near Kennedy Airport in the early 1960s for $1.6 million. Too late he realized he had overextended himself. Short the difference between the cost and the first mortgage, he had come to Gottlieb, desperately seeking investors so the bank would not foreclose on his mortgage. Gottlieb introduced him to Friedgood.

In March 1964 Friedgood visited the then incomplete Holiday Inn. He tramped with Miller through pilings and half-finished rooms, allowed Miller to buy him dinner, then decided to invest. He had his lawyer form a company for him and Sophie, which they called So-Char Realty, with him as president and her as treasurer. In April, with money earned from his practice, with Sophie's money from her parents, and with money whose origin he did not explain to Sophie, So-Char purchased a 45 percent share in the Holiday Inn for $450,000.

There was only one hitch. When it came time to sign, Friedgood did not appear. Miller and his attorneys waited for him through the day, placing calls to his home, his hospitals, his office. When finally he arrived for the closing, late that afternoon, Friedgood announced that—before he would sign—Miller must pay Gottlieb a finder's fee of $12,500. Friedgood told Miller to make the check out to his father, Heinrich Friedgood, instead of directly to Gottlieb. Miller was furious. He was also a businessman. Desperate to pay his creditors, he was in no position to question Friedgood's demands. He reluctantly agreed.

Despite this inauspicious start to their partnership, Miller and Friedgood appeared at first to be fast friends. Like Friedgood, Miller had also moved to Long Island's North Shore, just over the Suffolk County line in Huntington Bay, where he had built a glassed-in home on an exclusive stretch of beachfront with an expansive view of the bay. Outside he had planted heavy, lush shrubbery, all of which made the view from his living-room window out over his plants down to the water seem like the vista from a Caribbean Holiday Inn, incongruously translated to Long Island.

Miller and Friedgood visited each other regularly at their homes. Miller also appeared two or three times a week at Friedgood's office at Interboro Hospital to use the telephone and make his deals. But as so often happened with Friedgood, the relationship would end badly. Sooner or later everything may come down to money, but Miller may well have asked himself, At what price?

/ iii

As the children would remember it, their mother seemed to change after the move to Long Island. At first they attributed it to Kensington's influence. "I don't think she wanted to move," recalled Debbie, the youngest daughter, in the way she came to have of defending or justifying her mother's every action. In Brooklyn "my mother had just dropped in on neighbors. In Kensington social life was much more formal, and she felt she had to make an appointment." In Brooklyn she had never gone to a hairdresser. Now in Kensington she was suddenly aware of how her children looked, criticizing their clothes, poking painful fun at them.

Her concern about appearances extended even to their new housekeeper, a Dominican immigrant named Lydia Fernandez, who barely spoke English. Sophie seemed to have adopted Lydia. When the children were at school, she bought Lydia clothes and took her to the movies. But Lydia, the children remembered, never seemed to get her outfits right. She wore checks with stripes, or stripes with checks. Sophie would become furious and berate her.

Yet in retrospect the children would realize it was not Kensington that had changed their mother. Nor even the stroke—which, their father later delighted in telling people at his office, "altered my wife's personality."

"I remember the fights," said Toba, the oldest daughter, afterward. "Fighting about business stuff."

"We never knew the details," remembered Debbie, "but it always had to do with money. There was cheating and lawyers and that thing with Mr. Miller my mother would never tell us about."

And yet no matter what their father did, it seemed to the children their mother always forgave him. Once, at dinner, there was a bitter argument, with Sophie cursing and shouting at him. In front of them all she accused their father of not telling her the truth. To raise the rest of the money to invest with Miller in the Holiday Inn, she discovered, he had forged the children's signatures on bonds they had been given by her parents.

Later that evening, as Toba sat in her room puzzling over the argument and what her father had done, her mother entered. She sat down on Toba's bed and began to talk to her. "When it comes to money," she tried to explain, "your father is just a little boy. He has so many other virtues. Just give him a chance."

And always after they fought, the children remembered, their mother would say to them, "Did you speak to your father? Did you call him?" Perhaps, Toba would think, it was her mother's way of feeling that if as a father he needed the children, he also needed her as a wife.

But there was one fight the children never forgot, for it was the only time they ever saw their father strike their mother. They had all been in Michigan visiting their father's sister, with whom Chafke had been staying. From there they were to drive to Hazleton, where one of their mother's cousins was to be married. But as they prepared to leave, their father announced that Chafke was coming with them to Hazleton.

Sophie objected, saying there was no room in the car for her. They began to argue. Soon they were shouting at each other. "You can drive by yourself," Friedgood yelled at her as they walked out to the car. "I'm going with my mother back to New York."

Suddenly he pushed her. She fell to the ground. Stunned, she looked up at him and began to cry.

As though realizing he had gone too far, their father seemed to draw back. But by now Sophie was hysterical. She lay on the ground, sobbing, clutching her pocketbook, then took out items from it, one by one—her comb, her lipstick—and threw them feebly, desperately at him.

Finally, at the last minute, it seemed, their father

changed his mind. With Sophie still sobbing he announced that his mother would remain in Michigan. He would drive with them to Hazleton. And so they all took their places in the station wagon, their father driving, their mother next to him, David and Debbie in the back in the third seat, Stephen between the back and second seats, Toba in the middle seat, flanked by Esther and Beth.

As soon as they were driving, their parents began to sing. Sophie started with her favorite, "Bim-bom"; their father took over with "On the Road to Mandalay."

"On the road to Mandalay," he sang as they headed east to Pennsylvania,

> "Where the flying fishes play
> And the dawn comes up like thunder
> Out of China 'cross the bay."

Soon their parents were singing together, as though the fight had never occurred.

/ iv

Through all the fights, all the outbursts, Sophie confided in no one, least of all her children. "She never let us know her burdens because she didn't want us to pity her," explained Debbie—who more than any of them would become her mother's defender. "She never told us about our father or herself because she so desperately wanted to keep the family together."

Instead, to her daughters their mother appeared to be a superwoman. Except for that time in Michigan, Debbie remembered, "I only saw her cry once. It was Toba's birthday. We were all driving in New Hampshire when my father received a long-distance phone call from Pennsylvania.

"'Your father is seriously ill,'" he said when he returned from the telephone.

Of course there was no question of prolonging the family holiday; instead they began the all-day trip south to Hazleton, Sophie tense and anxious in the front seat. Only when they arrived that night did she learn the truth. Her father was not ill. He was dead. Even in front of the children she could not control herself. She cried bitterly.

/ v

And the fights between their parents continued. Now, though, when their mother became angry at their father, he would mimic her. "See, see, she's crazy," he would say in front of her to the children. And to the children it seemed she would take it out on them.

She began to criticize, to ridicule them. "I remember there was pinching, shouting, hitting," said Toba. "I remember how hard my mother was on my brother David because he was having trouble in school."

Toba was also having trouble. "I remember I almost failed French in my freshman year of high school. It became the bane of my existence because to my mother it meant I wouldn't get into a good college. Once, when I was given my report card, I didn't come home for three hours, I was so afraid."

She fared no better at the Old Westbury Country Club, which Friedgood and Sophie joined. Once the 530-acre estate of Harry Payne Whitney, it had boasted three swimming pools, three golf courses, polo fields, a glass-enclosed tennis house, gold-plated bathroom fixtures, and a 68-horse stable. It was now the preserve of wealthy Jewish doctors, lawyers, and businessmen.

Both Friedgood and Sophie had taken up golf. Although her stroke had left her with a slight limp, she was determined to overcome it and prided herself on being able to walk the two or three miles over the club's hilly course. She was no less determined to have her children enjoy the club with her.

Every weekend, it seemed, Sophie tried to bring Toba to the club with her. She wanted Toba, who was a teenager now, to meet the people there. They were rich people, Sophie would tell her. They were important. Maybe Toba might like one of their sons.

But Toba did not enjoy the country club. She was shy, overweight, and self-conscious. And when she refused to go, Sophie began to ridicule her. "Creep, cowface, horseface," Sophie would shout at her. "Later she would say she was sorry, that she didn't mean it," Toba remembered later. "But looking back on it I know I felt a lot of self-hate."

Sophie even began to ridicule the baby, Debbie. "When I turned twelve or thirteen," says Debbie now, "I gained a lot of weight, and my relationship with my mother changed drastically." The same words Sophie used to Toba, she now used to Debbie.

Sometimes she became angry because Debbie's hair was frizzy or because she had a hole in her jeans. Once she caught Debbie smoking and made her swallow an entire pack of cigarettes. Another time, enraged over some shortcoming, she began slapping her daughter uncontrollably. Debbie ran and hid in a closet and cried and cried. To spite her mother she refused to comb her hair or wear dresses. "I thought she hated me. From fourteen to nineteen I despised her."

It was only Esther that Sophie seemed to care for. Fair-skinned, blond, and petite, Esther had poise, a confidence and coolness that her sisters lacked. She sang. She danced. She painted. Alone among them, Esther cared about clothes. Alone among them, Esther loved going with her mother to the Old Westbury Country Club. Often Sophie would say to her other daughters, "Esther is more like me than any of you. When I was a girl, I was an Esther."

"My mother had high goals and didn't tolerate weakness in people," Esther—her mother's favorite, or so they all thought at the time—would explain afterward. "When she insulted Toba, Toba would cry and feel bad and would take it because she had a low opinion of herself. I was a lot more aggressive. I am strong and don't tolerate weakness in people. I was never the 'horseface.' I was never the 'cowface.' "

And so, shut out of their mother's good graces, Toba and Debbie turned to their father. As a little girl in Brooklyn, Toba, as the eldest daughter, had been permitted to accompany him each Sunday morning to his office on Eastern Parkway. Because she was the doctor's daughter, she had been special to his nurses, to his patients. She had arranged her father's file cards like a secretary. She had watched his patients adore him and she had adored him as well.

Now—as he did with his poor patients, with Blackie, with Suzie Bren, with Suzie Bren's cousin—Friedgood supported, comforted his daughters. "Don't listen to her," he said to them of their mother when she shouted at them. "She's upset, she doesn't mean it."

Instead he always complimented them. "He gave us confidence," remembered Debbie. "He could make you believe you were great." Whenever Debbie went out at night on a date, he would leave her a note in her wallet. "Have a good time," he would write. "Love, Papa."

Unlike Sophie, he never became angry at them. And because he never became angry, because he never raised his voice at them, they looked at him, as Debbie remembered later, "as their savior." When Sophie shouted at him, when she embarrassed him in front of people, he never spoke, never expressed any emotion. "Instead," remembered Debbie, "his face would go through contortions, and my heart would contort for him."

9

IN THE SPRING OF 1967 CHARLES FRIEDGOOD MET
Harriet Boell Larsen. Later, when she had achieved a certain
degree of notoriety, the tabloid newspapers would deliciously
describe her as "the Danish Pastry," but by no stretch of the
imagination could Harriet Larsen be thought of as a beautiful
woman. She was stylish, perhaps; young, certainly. When
Friedgood met her she was working as a nurse in the operating room at Interboro Hospital, having come to the hospital
earlier that year from Denmark with three other nurses.

She had grown up in the small southern Danish town of
Tøender, near the German border. Her parents had divorced
and she had been reared by her mother, who fancied herself
something of an artist. According to her roommate at the hospital, Lena Morowski, Harriet had come to the States after the
breakup of her romance with a young Danish doctor. At the
time, Harriet was twenty-eight years old, and pregnant. When
the young Danish doctor decided not to marry her, she had an
abortion that left her, as Lena put it, "depressed for half a year
afterward." She was so sensitive about it, Lena recalled, that
whenever the subject of children came up she would have to

leave the room; perhaps she thought she could leave all that pain behind her when she came to America.

Harriet, Lena, and two other nurses all found work at Interboro, and Harriet and Lena shared an apartment across the street. Soon after arriving at Interboro, Harriet fell in love with the chief of surgery. For hours, it seemed, she would sit in her apartment, her small dog in her lap, in a rocking chair by the window. From there she could see the hospital, the doctors coming and going. Whenever she saw the chief surgeon coming out, she would rush over to the mirror, straighten her hair, take the dog out for a walk, and casually bump into him.

The romance never flowered, however, and she soon took up with another doctor, who was separated from his wife. That romance also foundered. She took up with a third doctor, whose reputation was that he had approached every nurse at the hospital. There was nothing there for her, either.

Then, one day, in the hospital cafeteria, when Harriet, in her white uniform, was sitting by herself, an old woman approached her. "You're a nurse?" the woman asked her in a heavy Yiddish accent. "My son is a doctor. He is looking for a nurse." It was Chafke Friedgood.

As he had done with his other workers, Friedgood at first paid Harriet off the books. But unlike the others, Harriet Larsen was an educated woman, a qualified nurse. She insisted on cleaning his instruments. She knew how to give injections. Soon she was running his office. Later, when he was not there, she even wrote out his prescriptions and examined his patients.

Now Friedgood began to change. No longer did he stay at his office past midnight, treating patients. Harriet would not permit him to stay past nine or ten o'clock at the latest. His appearance also changed. Blackie and Suzie Bren smiled to each other as they noticed he now wore a doctor's white coat. His shoes were shined. His jacket matched his pants. And when his graying curly hair grew long, Harriet would badger him, "Charlie, you need a haircut."

Working with him, Harriet began keeping his irregular hours. She made hospital rounds with him. Late at night, when they were finished, they would have dinner. Seeing them together, Suzie Bren would notice how much more relaxed the doctor seemed; how good they seemed for each other; how he seemed happier now than she had ever remembered him.

Nor was she the only person to notice the change in Friedgood. One snowy afternoon, after he and Harriet had made their hospital rounds together, one of his patients happened to look out his window. He saw the two of them, Dr. Friedgood and his nurse, walking back to the doctor's car. They were laughing and throwing snowballs at each other.

A few weeks after Harriet began working for him, she said to her roommate, Lena, "Charlie is the type of person you'd love to have as a father." Later she would actually refer to him as "Daddy." Still later, the term she would use for him was *Konge,* the Danish word for "king."

/ ii

At first Harriet told no one of their relationship. In front of others, neither of them displayed any emotion, any affection toward the other. Harriet would not admit, even to Lena, that there was anything serious between them. Only to the third Danish nurse, Inge Pingel, did she confide she was "seeing someone." And she didn't confess to her until a year later that it was Friedgood. Inge learned of the relationship when she slept at Harriet's apartment one night when Lena was not there. "I guess I'll have to tell you my secret since you're going to stay here," Harriet said to her. Harriet asked Inge to sleep on the couch in the living room so Friedgood could sleep with her.

When he visited Harriet and Lena's apartment, Harriet would give him lessons in Danish. He seemed to take great pride, Lena recalled, in learning the words, and would try out his vocabulary on each of the girls. But Lena did not approve of the relationship. Once, when she and Harriet were talking in Danish about Harriet's parents, Harriet suddenly referred to Friedgood in English as "Daddy." A mature girl of twenty-eight calling this man Daddy! Lena was annoyed.

Harriet maintained to Lena and Inge that she had made up her mind never to marry, but, says Inge, "She was determined to have children."

"If I don't find the right man to marry," Harriet said to Inge, "I will have children when I am thirty nevertheless." She would find an "intelligent" person; she would look for "genes." "The only thing I want of him is that he would be the father of my children."

By the time Harriet turned thirty the man she was involved with was Friedgood. "Don't do it," Lena warned her. "Give yourself another year. Date someone your own age." Inge reminded Harriet how when she met her own husband, Ole—who had been a Danish soccer star in Denmark and then followed Inge to the United States—Harriet had counseled her not to see him, saying that to do so was wrong because Ole was already married and it was unfair to Ole's wife. But now when Inge gave the same advice to her, Harriet said it was "different." They did not speak again for a year.

/ iii

As Harriet's relationship with Friedgood deepened, the question of marriage arose more and more frequently. But there was an impediment: Sophie. To Harriet, Friedgood described his wife as a crazy woman, someone who was not normal, someone who belonged in a psychiatric hospital. "She should not live in society," he told her, "but behind bars someplace."

Together they would call her "crazy Sophie" and laugh—an intimate joke between them.

It was the stroke, Friedgood told Harriet, that accounted for his wife's bizarre behavior. It had altered her entire personality—so drastically, he said, that her own children despised her. Sometimes, trying to soothe Harriet, he spoke of divorcing Sophie. But always he would add that she would never give him a divorce if she found out about them. There was money he had invested with Sophie, lots of money, hundreds of thousands of dollars. If Sophie found out about them, he told Harriet, he would never be able to touch it.

Despite these warnings and apprehensions, Friedgood insisted on bringing Harriet with him to Kensington. One Friday evening, while Sophie and the children waited for him to begin the *Shabbos* dinner, he appeared with her. "This is my nurse," he said to his wife and children of the tall young blond woman standing by his side. "She is from Denmark. She has no family or friends, and is alone in a strange new country."

Later on, when Sophie or the children asked him about her, he told them different stories. She was married, he said to them once, but her husband—like his own father—was a traveling salesman and never at home. Another time, Harriet's ex-lover, the young Danish doctor, visited the United States, and Friedgood brought him to Kensington with Harriet. Friedgood introduced the young man to his family as Harriet's fiancé.

Knowing how Sophie abused Toba and Debbie and how they turned to him for comfort, he now felt he could take them into his confidence. Often, when they were out driving together, the three of them, he would say, "Why don't we stop off and see Harriet for a little bit?" And then he would always add, "But don't tell your mother."

The two girls began to look forward to visiting Harriet. Often she would make them lunch or dinner, and the girls would ask her if she and their father would get married and allow them to live with them, instead of with Sophie. Soon both girls were deeply enmeshed in the affair. When Toba returned home for Christmas vacation after her freshman year in college, and her father met her at the Great Neck railroad station, the first thing they did was to stop off and visit Harriet before driving home. When the family was about to leave on a trip, and Friedgood told Sophie he was leaving his car at a nearby garage for repairs while they were away, he told Toba to follow him in the second car so that she could pick him up, and instead of taking the first car to the garage, they left it at Harriet's.

When they returned home, Sophie was waiting at the front door. "Where were you? What took you so long?" she demanded of Toba, who had entered the house while her father was parking the car in the driveway.

"Oh," explained Toba, "Papa took the car to Harriet's."

Moments later, when Friedgood came into the house, Toba heard her mother questioning him. "You didn't tell me you were going to Harriet's," her mother shouted.

"Harriet?" her father answered. "I don't know what you're talking about."

When Debbie was graduated from junior high, Sophie threw a party for her. But as he was accustomed to doing when it came to family celebrations, Friedgood did not come on time. Not until an hour later, in the midst of the celebration, did he arrive. With him was Harriet.

Seeing them standing quietly together, her husband and this tall young blond woman, Sophie froze. In front of everyone, in front of all Debbie's friends, she began to scream at Harriet. "Bitch!" she shouted at her. "Whore!" She began walking toward them. Suddenly, reaching down, she pulled off her shoe, then flung it at Harriet.

Terrified of her mother, protective of her father, herself an overweight and insecure teenager, Debbie was humiliated. Her mother, she thought, was brutal. And through it all her father said nothing. He only smiled.

Years later, after Debbie had married and she and her husband were living in a two-room walk-up in New York City, she would tell the story—a tormented young woman, pouring out these sad, ugly details one after another. "Because I was so angry at my mother in those years, I was fond of Harriet. I would write my father poetry and write Harriet long, intimate letters. Later, when she became pregnant, I wrote her a letter complimenting her on her 'maturing belly.' I wanted my father to run away with her. I thought of her as this wonderful woman who is making my dear, sweet father so happy."

Suddenly, as she spoke, she looked away. When she turned back, her eyes were filled with tears. "Only later did I realize it was my mother who really loved me."

10

IN 1971, FOUR YEARS AFTER SHE MET FRIEDGOOD, Harriet became pregnant. At first she and Friedgood tried to hide the fact. Harriet told her friends the father was her former Danish fiancé, the young doctor.

At the end of the year she left for Denmark. Early in 1972 she gave birth to a boy, a curly-haired, blond little boy who was the image of Friedgood. In the custom of the Jewish religion he insisted the child be named after a deceased relative. The name he chose was Heinrich—that of his own deceased father.

Three months later, Harriet returned to the United States. Now friends noticed a change in their relationship. They seemed to have become closer, more intimate. Before, Harriet had given the impression she only wanted a child and then would return to Denmark. Now she spoke differently.

For the first time Harriet talked of having a family of her own, "a normal family," as she put it. No longer did she want to work as a nurse. "Stop working and have kids," she would tell Inge and Lena, both of whom were now married. "She even talked of having another child," Lena recalled, "and of having a big family as well."

At Friedgood's request, Harriet began to study Judaism.
Later that year, when she attended the hospital's Christmas
party, Friedgood objected. And when she attended a Christmas party at Inge and Ole Pingel's, Friedgood insisted she
bring her own food because the Pingels might serve pork.

At first when she returned to the United States with the
baby there was a problem about where she would stay. At first
Friedgood put her up at the Holiday Inn near Kennedy Airport. But Harriet was not happy there. For a brief time she
moved in with Inge and Ole. She liked that no better. Finally
Friedgood found her an apartment in Bayside, Queens, just a
few minutes' drive from Kensington, a high-rise with a balcony that overlooked the Cross-Island Parkway and Long Island
Sound. To pay her rent, to care for his son, he began paying
her an allowance of a thousand dollars a month.

Though he had not found the time to do it for his other
children, Friedgood would help Harriet bathe and care for the
baby. She needed help, in fact, for she had not been able to
stop working, as she wished. Instead she continued as Friedgood's nurse, running his office. Sometimes she would bring
little Heinrich with her to work. Then Friedgood would take
the boy in his arms and announce smilingly to his receptionists
and patients alike, "Look, look, give a look at this! Isn't he
beautiful?"

Clearly Friedgood was as pleased with his son as was
Harriet. "Doesn't he look like me?" Inge's husband, Ole,
would remember Friedgood asking him whenever he and
Harriet came for a visit. And Friedgood would take the little
boy in his arms, lift him high above his head, and smile adoringly at him.

There is a picture of Friedgood with his son at Harriet's
apartment. He is standing on the balcony, the parkway and
the Sound in the distance. His face is full, his now-gray hair
curly, and he is holding little Heinrich, with his beautiful
blond curls, gently and proudly in his arms.

When Chafke came to the office, he would show Hein-

rich to her, though he would not admit to her that the child
was his or even that Harriet was his mother. At first the old
lady refused to acknowledge the boy or her son's relationship
with Harriet. Yet time after time, in her son's office, seeing the
little boy laughing and smiling, seeing how his face resembled
that of her own son, and hers as well, she could not help being
touched. In a backhanded way she acknowledged their kin-
ship by sending Harriet a newspaper clipping, a "Dear Abby"
or Ann Landers column of advice to a reader. "A daughter-in-
law must love her mother-in-law," said the column in bold-
faced type. "Otherwise she cannot love her husband."

Now, as her son and Harriet made their rounds of the
hospitals together, she began to baby-sit for them. Sometimes
Friedgood would pack his mother and the baby into the car
with them when he and Harriet made their rounds. While he
and Harriet went off to see his patients his mother would sit in
the car and mind the boy.

/ ii

But for Friedgood there were still problems—not just with Sophie, but money problems, too. No matter how much money
he earned from his practice, no matter how much money Sophie had of her own, he always seemed in debt. "I have to be
careful of asking him for too much money," Harriet would tell
her friends, "because he is under such a financial strain." It
was true. Six months after Heinrich was born, Friedgood went
on trial for income-tax evasion.

The Internal Revenue Service's investigation of him
had begun soon after his indictment for performing abortions
during the years 1961 to 1964. In 1962 Friedgood had reported taxable income of $14,150. In 1963 he had reported
$38,611. In 1964, $34,779. Knowing he might have received
thousands of dollars in illegal, unreported abortion fees, the
IRS began checking his tax returns for those years.

The investigation had begun in 1965, with a letter to Friedgood asking specific questions about his returns. Friedgood did not respond. In February 1966 he received a second letter. Two months later the IRS received a reply citing "inadvertent omission of income for the years 1962–64." Friedgood, his attorney explained, "had a very busy medical practice and did not have time to maintain adequate financial records." Enclosed in the letter was an unsolicited check to the IRS for $25,000.

It took the IRS five more years to examine Friedgood's tax returns for those three years. By then they discovered that to help pay for his business investments, Friedgood had each year diverted $100,000 from his medical fees to a separate bank account in his father's name. From it he would write checks in his father's name without informing the old man. Nor, when filing his income-tax returns, did he inform his accountant.

In 1971 Friedgood was indicted on three counts of income-tax evasion. For 1962, the government concluded, his taxable income was not $14,150, as he had reported it; it was $105,473. For 1963 it was not $38,611; it was $131,645. For 1964 it was not $34,779; it was $119,205. In all, with interest payments, he owed the government nearly $400,000.

As he had done for his abortion trial, Friedgood hired the best legal counsel. This time his attorney was Mike Gillen—Irish, street-smart, and a former federal prosecutor who had made something of a reputation by obtaining the bank-robbery conviction of a Long Island *mafioso* named Sonny Franzese. "Tough guys, assassins, violent men" was the way Gillen described the people whom he had prosecuted, then later defended. Yet in all his criminal-law experience, he would say afterward, he had never come across anyone like Charles Friedgood.

"He'd tell you bullshit story after bullshit story," Gillen recalled. "He'd smile. He never lost his temper. He never showed any emotion. No rage. No anger. Nothing seemed to bother him at all. He lived in a world all his own.

"What amazed me was that this was a healer, an educated man. Yet no tough guy I ever defended could get people to perjure themselves the way Charlie Friedgood did. People were willing to lie their heads off for him. He had all these guys, these rabbis with the *tzitzis,* who made up the same stories he did."

There had been one rabbi in particular who had seemed to Gillen like "a decent guy." He was a little old man who wore a long black coat, a dark beard, and *tzitzis*—the picture of a holy man, Gillen had thought. Before allowing him to testify, Gillen had first questioned the rabbi in his office. The rabbi, the picture of holiness, had sworn to Gillen he would tell the truth.

"You say you knew Dr. Friedgood's father?" Gillen began.

"Oh, yes," answered the rabbi.

"How long would you say you knew him?" Gillen asked.

"For years," said the rabbi.

"Rabbi," said Gillen, "can you describe the doctor's father?"

"Can I meet him first?"

/ iii

The trial began in September 1972, in Brooklyn Federal Court. Every morning it was the same, Friedgood appearing in court, smiling, arm-in-arm with Sophie. Throughout the trial he sat next to her, calm and expressionless. During the noon recess he would rush out the door to one of his hospitals, where he had just enough time to perform an operation before court resumed in the afternoon.

Against this image of professional unimpeachability and personal substance—this portrait of a man so upright and so wealthy that tax evasion would never occur to him—the prosecution could only present facts. The government had subpoenaed executives of Blue Shield and Blue Cross—two of the many medical plans that paid the bills of most of Friedgood's patients—to question them about the fees he had received. As they were about to testify two four-wheel dollies were brought into the courtroom. On them were copies of printouts of checks to Friedgood for the years 1962–64. There were so many that each dolly weighed over one hundred pounds, the piles of printouts reaching three feet into the air. In those three years Friedgood had, it appeared, performed literally thousands upon thousands of operations.

Now, one by one, the executives were called to the stand. Because he had performed so many operations, they testified, Friedgood had been on a special list of doctors who were checked for each bill they submitted to the companies for payment. By 1962 he had filed so many claims that every form he submitted was automatically kicked out of the computer so that Blue Cross/Blue Shield's medical staff could ensure they were not fraudulent.

Seeing the dollies wheeled into the courtroom, listening to the Blue Shield executives' testimony, Sophie turned to Gillen. "It doesn't look good for Charles, does it?" she said.

Friedgood's defense—a not-uncommon one in income-tax trials—was that he was not responsible for filing false income-tax returns; someone else was; in Friedgood's case, his now deceased father, Ichy. Ichy, who had barely eked out a living selling closeout items; who had sat in his son's office selling socks, shirts, and ties to patients for a quarter or fifty cents—the same Ichy was responsible, Friedgood claimed, for underestimating his income tax by more than a quarter of a million dollars. He himself, operating day and night, had had no idea what the old man was about.

As the centerpiece of his defense, Friedgood himself took the witness stand. In his rumpled suit, his curly hair in disarray and needing a trim, his thick glasses, he projected the air of the dedicated, if distracted, professor.

"Dr. Friedgood," began Gillen, striking a serious pose, "would you tell us, please, your medical background?"

"My medical degree," Friedgood answered calmly, skipping over his dismissal from the University of Michigan, "was from Wayne State University in 1946.... My postgraduate training consisted of an internship at Detroit Receiving Hospital; and residence in surgery at the University of Pennsylvania Hospital. I was then," he grandiloquently announced, "chief resident in surgery at Mount Sinai Hospital in New York City."

"And what did you do after your residency?" asked Gillen.

"I then," Friedgood continued, neglecting to mention his dismissals from Maimonides, from Beth El, and from the other hospitals, "took a job as an associate professor of surgery at Downstate Medical Center in Brooklyn, and was associate director at Maimonides Hospital in Brooklyn."

The defendant's bona fides established, Gillen turned to the subject of Friedgood's father. "Was your father a man of financial substance, Dr. Friedgood?"

"Yes," Friedgood answered. "He was always independent. He had the means to live the way he liked. He never had any problems financially, even during the Depression. He always made a living. He owned three stores and we had our own home.... His gift to his grandchildren," he announced, "was to send them to summer camp."

"Your grandparents, were they—where did they live?" asked Gillen.

"In Israel," Friedgood answered.

"Did any moneys come to your father from your grandfather?"

"Oh, yes."

"How much?"

"Well," Friedgood began, "according to Jewish law, the older son inherits the estate. We, my father, being the oldest son, he inherited all the properties in Israel."

"What kind of properties were in Israel?"

"There were quite a few houses . . . commercial proper-ties, a lot of acreage, land which subsequently became valu-able property." More valuable, no doubt, than the Friedgood apartment on LaSalle Boulevard in Detroit.

After a month-long trial the jury found Friedgood guilty. To keep him from jail, Gillen offered an elegant, if disingenuous, peroration before the judge. "There stands before the court now," he began, "a physician who became a physician through many years of study—I need not remind the court of how many years of formal education and of course internship and residencies and things of that nature. . . . He is a surgeon, which I believe is a step higher than most doctors attain. His credentials are of the highest. . . . He has given a lifetime of service to the community. He operates in areas in the city where it is dangerous to life to work, and yet this man goes in to perform these operations, where other doctors have abso-lutely refused. . . . And there are many people in this city that just can't afford the type of help Dr. Friedgood has been giv-ing for years. . . ."

Pleading for leniency for himself, Friedgood broke into tears. "I want to ask for mercy for the innocent victims, my wife and my six children," he begged. "I would appreciate it if you could see mercy in your heart to let me avoid jail. I will make amends. The government will not lose any money from taxes. I will pay back every cent as long as I am alive and able to work."

Gillen's presentation worked. His client was ordered to pay his back taxes, put on probation for five years, and sent to a public-health facility in Texas (where Harriet visited him each weekend) for a month. And rather than pay every cent, he began putting his remaining assets—including his shares in So-Char Realty—in Sophie's name.

But Gillen was not quite finished with Friedgood. "He wanted me to appeal," said Gillen later, "but he wanted me to appeal for him on the cuff. He was too cheap to pay for a new trial." Gillen filed the appeal. But Friedgood never paid him. Said Gillen, "He stiffed me."

/ iv

Then, as if the trials and the pressures of his double life had begun to erode the facade Friedgood had constructed, an extraordinary event occurred—an event so bizarre, revealing something so appalling, so frightening, that Sophie could not bring herself ever to tell her children or her friends. It was as though her husband had lost control over himself, as though the impulses that had led his college chum Edward Rosen to call him a sociopath were now fully exposed.

Exactly how or why his dispute with Toby Miller began is not clear. But by early 1970 Friedgood was convinced that his partner in the Holiday Inn franchise was cheating him. Miller protested, but Friedgood continued to suspect him. So, to settle their differences, they entered into a complicated buy-sell agreement over their shares in the Holiday Inn enterprise: the agreement specified that either partner had the option to buy out the other at a fixed price and that, if the seller was not satisfied with the other partner's offer, he had the option of countering within thirty days at a price 10 percent above the original offer.

The agreement contained a final item. If either party defaulted as purchaser, the seller could then repurchase his partner's interest at his original offer. The key, then, was liquidity, the ability of either party to lay his hands quickly on enough money to meet the purchase price. Miller, an experienced businessman, was aware of this; Friedgood was not.

Since the mid-1960s, when they had gone into partnership together, the value of their Holiday Inn had increased substantially—some put the figure at over $2 million. It was in the summer of 1972 that Miller made his offer to Friedgood. For Friedgood's 45 percent interest, for which he had originally paid $450,000 more than eight years before, Miller now offered him $400,000.

Friedgood rejected this sum and counteroffered with 10 percent more. It was here the trouble began, for he could not come up with the money. Miller then claimed Friedgood had defaulted and that his own original offer of $400,000 still held.

Friedgood tried to contact Miller, to discuss the matter with him. For weeks Friedgood tried to reach him. But Miller now refused to talk. Friedgood then asked Harriet to call Miller, to say she was a contractor and to offer him money if he would meet with her at the Holiday Inn. But Harriet was afraid to. Instead she asked Inge. Inge was also afraid.

Late in the morning of July 2, 1972, Miller's attorney received a telephone call at his office in Mineola. It was Miller, who was hysterical. "Come to my house!" he shouted, out of breath, his words slurred. "Charlie Friedgood! Charlie Friedgood tried to kill me! He's here now. Come quickly!"

Forty minutes later the attorney arrived at Miller's home in Huntington Bay. Miller's face was bruised, his nose bleeding. He seemed dazed. Friedgood was nowhere in sight.

Horrified and incredulous, the attorney tried to find out what had happened, and gradually pieced together a bizarre story. He had left his home that morning at eight A.M. in his new Mercedes-Benz, Miller began. As he backed out of his driveway and turned onto the secluded dirt road that led to the main thoroughfare, he noticed another car, a blue Mustang, he thought, parked outside his house. About fifty feet down the road he saw another car, a gold Cadillac with a dark vinyl roof, parked across the road. The Cadillac appeared to be disabled. Miller pulled his Mercedes alongside it and stopped.

A husky young man with dark hair and heavy sideburns

approached and asked where the nearest service station was. As Miller lowered his window to answer, the husky young man yanked open his car door, pushed Miller across to the passenger side, then sat down in the driver's seat.

With that, Miller said, a second man appeared at the window. "Do you know Charlie Friedgood, Toby?" he said to Miller. "Who did you swindle today, Toby?"

Then Miller saw the blue Mustang pull up, and out of it stepped Friedgood. Carrying a brown envelope in one hand, he walked over to Miller's car, opened the door on the passenger side, and got inside, pushing Miller into the middle. "These fellows won't hurt you, Toby," he said. "Let's find a quiet place to talk. I have some papers for you."

The husky man started up the car as Miller directed him to a driveway about three hundred feet away. It was a long, wide driveway with grass in the middle, Miller remembered. They pulled the car in about twenty feet and stopped. Friedgood and the second man stepped out of the car.

"Give me your jacket," Friedgood said to Miller. Suddenly the two men began to pull Miller's jacket off. When Miller looked up, Friedgood was standing over him, the door to the Mercedes open. In his right hand Friedgood had a hypodermic syringe, in his left, a vial. He was holding up the syringe, filling it.

"What are you doing, Charlie? What have you got there?"

"Don't worry. It will put you to sleep and make you groggy for a while. Raise your right arm."

Friedgood leaned into the car and gave Miller an injection below his right armpit. He then produced a batch of typewritten papers and legal forms, including what Miller believed were promissory notes in what appeared to be Friedgood's handwriting. One of the notes, Miller saw, was for $255,000.

"Sign these papers and the notes," Friedgood ordered.

"What are they, Charlie?"

"Never mind what they are," said Friedgood.

"Don't read them," said the husky man. "Just sign your name if you know what's good for you."

Miller signed everything Friedgood put before him. In all, he remembered, he signed his name twelve to fifteen times. "Charlie's my uncle, so don't try to swindle or cheat him out of anything or we'll take care of you," said the husky man. "We're letting you off easy this time. We're going to get out of here. You'll find your keys in the dirt."

By now, Miller said, he was feeling dizzy. He could not get out of his car. Instead he sat and stared straight ahead. Moments later Friedgood reappeared. He got back into the Mercedes in the driver's seat. In his hand were Miller's keys. "Please, Charlie," Miller managed to say. "Please drive me home."

The next thing Miller remembered was awakening for a moment in a chair in his living room, with Friedgood sitting next to him. He dozed off again. This time he was awakened by someone hitting him on his head, pounding him in the chest and the face, shouting and cursing at him. "I'm going to kill you," the person was shouting. "I'm going to kill you." Miller looked up. It was Friedgood. They began to struggle. Though Miller was shorter and lighter than Friedgood, and still groggy from the injection, the former athlete was able to fight the doctor off. Finally he persuaded him to call their attorney to mediate whatever disagreements they had.

But when the attorney arrived an hour later, Friedgood had gone. Seeing Miller bruised and bleeding, the attorney rushed his client to the emergency room of nearby Huntington Hospital. Miller was hurried to the intensive-care unit, where he remained four days. For the first day he was on the critical list. Four days later he was moved out of intensive care into a regular room. Not until a week later was he released from the hospital.

He then filed a complaint against Friedgood with the Suffolk County police. The case was investigated by Detective Allen Watterson of the department's Second Squad in Huntington. From Miller, Watterson obtained photographs of the scene, of himself still bruised, and of the bloodied clothes he had worn on the day of his attack. From Huntington Hospital he obtained the record of the admitting doctor's initial report of a puncture wound under Miller's right armpit. From the hospital's associate pathologist he obtained the analysis of Miller's blood and urine specimens done on the date of his admission. The tests showed a barbiturate presence of 4.7 milligrams, a nearly toxic amount.

At nine-thirty on the night of July 24, 1972, Friedgood was arrested at his home in Kensington and charged with assault, robbery, and kidnapping. He was taken to the Second Precinct, where he remained overnight. The following morning he was arraigned before First District Court Judge Victor J. Orgera, who ordered a psychiatric examination of him. On July 28 two psychiatrists, Dr. James V. Diodato and Dr. Irving Jacobs, examined him at Central Islip State Hospital. After a forty-five-minute joint interview they concluded that Friedgood did "not as a result of mental disease or defect lack capacity to understand the proceedings against him."

On September 27 the case, with all this information, was sent to the grand jury. But Friedgood was never indicted. Despite the evidence, Miller's story lacked a corroborating witness, and the grand jurors felt the tale was simply too far-fetched to be believed.

Once again, Friedgood was allowed to continue.

11

WHILE CHARLES FRIEDGOOD WAS STRUGGLING
with the law, Sophie was struggling with her daughters. Toba,
her eldest, had become an attractive young woman. She was
dark, with long hair, and, like her mother, tended to be on the
heavy side. Yet, unlike her mother, she had a gentleness, a
softness about her. Her sisters saw this softness as a weakness,
for she allowed herself to be swayed, even bullied, by her
mother. She had turned to her father and Harriet to escape
her mother, yet part of her still sought her mother's approval.
She didn't get it, and by the time she went off to college, at
age eighteen, she and Sophie were, as Toba put it years later,
"locked into a conflict." The conflict deepened when, in her
first year at the University of Toledo, she met Larry Press.

Just as she had pushed and prodded her daughter in
school, and at the Old Westbury Country Club, Sophie now
wanted Toba to meet an eligible young man, to marry well,
"to be financially successful." Larry Press did not fit into that
plan. Making money seemed the furthest thing from his mind.
He wore his hair in a ponytail. He drove a motorcycle. He refused to wear a tie or a suit—if, indeed, he owned one. Rather

than financial success, he wanted only to work with juvenile delinquents. Marriage, families, he told Toba, were "irrelevant." Larry Press was, in short, everything her mother disapproved of. Toba fell in love with him.

Sophie was horrified. To her, as she berated Toba, Larry Press was nothing but "a bum." Although she loved Larry, Toba was persuaded to transfer after her freshman year to Syracuse University, which later her sisters Esther and Beth also attended. Over the next three years, despite her mother's opposition, she and Larry Press continued to see each other. After her graduation they both moved to Cambridge, Massachusetts. There, in the early 1970s, among college students, street people, and the last of the flower children, they began to live together.

Again Sophie was horrified. She began to plot ways in which she could rescue Toba from Larry Press. At three o'clock one Saturday morning Toba and Larry were awakened in their apartment by loud banging on their front door. Toba opened the door to find her parents standing on the threshold. "Your grandmother is dying," her father said to her softly. "You have to come home immediately."

As her parents stood silently in the living room watching her, Toba began to pack her clothes. Suddenly Larry began shouting at her, "Toba, what's the matter with you? Can't you see your father is lying?" Toba turned and looked at her father. Only then did she understand.

The following year her sister Beth became engaged to a medical student, and plans were made for an elaborate wedding. At first Sophie refused to allow Toba to be part of the ceremony, but finally she changed her mind. Toba came down to New York and went to a large department store with her mother to be fitted for the gown Beth had chosen for her bridesmaids. Suddenly Sophie appeared to lose control of herself. "Bitch! Whore!" she began to sob at Toba in the middle of the store, with all the saleswomen standing there with their tape measures. "I don't have a daughter anymore."

Somehow, after the wedding, Sophie again persuaded Toba to leave Larry Press and return to New York. Toba found her own apartment in the city. Her father helped her obtain a job teaching English at one of the *yeshivas* he knew in Brooklyn. It was an all-girls' school, and Toba seemed happy there. The girls loved her. Outside of class she discussed sex with them and told them of her own first love. The girls saw her as an older sister.

And for the first time in her life she began to develop a relationship with her mother. "As I got more confidence, as I reached twenty-one or twenty-two," she would explain years later, "I began to relate to my mother as a woman." One Wednesday afternoon she took her girls to a Broadway musical, *Gentlemen Prefer Blondes,* and brought Sophie along with them. "The kids," she remembered, "loved my mother." After the show Sophie stayed in town to have dinner with Debbie, who had recently married and was also living in the city. Never, Debbie remembered, had she seen her mother so happy. Through dinner her mother was humming all the songs from the show. In the bathroom Debbie could hear her mother singing "Diamonds Are a Girl's Best Friend."

On weekends Toba would return to Kensington. After she would come home from a date with a young man that she felt her mother would approve of—a lawyer, a young businessman, even a medical student—she and Sophie would have a long talk. Late at night, after her father had long since gone to bed, Sophie would come into Toba's room. Sophie's hair would be all combed out, streaming down the back of her bathrobe. To Toba her mother looked beautiful.

They would talk about college, and Sophie would tell Toba about her own college days at Temple in Philadelphia, about men she had gone out, with before she met Charlie, and how she wanted Toba to make sure she married the right person. They would sit on the bed, Indian style, Toba remembered, and they would talk about everything until seven in the morning.

Everything, Toba sensed, but Sophie and her unhappiness with her husband. "About herself my mother would never let you penetrate. About herself my mother couldn't be honest."

After Toba had taught for a year, Sophie persuaded her to take the Law School Aptitude Tests, or LSATs, so she could enter law school. "That way you can meet another man," she told her. Toba took the LSATs. But she never went to law school. Instead she decided to marry Larry Press. When finally she got up the courage to tell her mother, Sophie objected so strenuously that Toba and Larry decided to elope.

The fleeting closeness Toba had felt with her mother was over. When she and Larry wanted to make a down payment on a house and asked Sophie for her fifty thousand dollars from a trust fund, started by Sophie's parents, which each daughter was to receive at age twenty-one, Sophie refused to give it to her.

Soon afterward Toba and Larry left New York for California.

/ ii

Debbie's relationship with her mother went through a similar metamorphosis. Vivacious and creative, yet—like Toba—filled with doubts about herself, she had become something of a free spirit. She wrote poetry. She took modern dance. Alone among her sisters, she refused to attend Syracuse University. Instead she entered Bard, a small liberal-arts college up the Hudson. After two years, when she was nineteen, she dropped out and returned to live in the city. One day she was riding in a taxi and struck up a conversation with the cabby. A few years older than she, he was an Egyptian Jew whose father had died when he was a boy. Penniless, he had come to the United States with his brother and his mother, who had struggled to support them. He was living in the East Village, in a two-room, sixth-floor walk-up apartment, driving a taxi while trying to establish himself as a photographer. Looking at his picture on the dashboard, Debbie saw a dark, bearded, brooding face and, below it, his name, Avi Menasche. Taking a pen from her pocketbook, she wrote it down on the back of her hand. The next day she telephoned him. "He was," she said afterward, "the first man I felt ever loved me."

Six months later they were married.

At first Debbie had taken Avi with her to Harriet's when she baby-sat for little Heinrich. At her father's urgings, Avi had even taken photographs of him and Harriet with the baby. But with her marriage, Debbie's relationship with her mother began to alter. On the surface Avi was everything Sophie professed to despise. He was poor. He dressed in sandals and jeans. In the apartment he and Debbie shared, burlap served for wallpaper, cushions for chairs. Nor did he want to better himself, to succeed as Sophie envisioned success. His pictures, of poor and handicapped children, displayed a sensitivity too painful for commercial appeal. And instead of profits, Avi talked of honesty and integrity.

Yet Sophie took a liking to him, and he did to her. "Avi had experienced pain all his life," Debbie would struggle—not fully successfully—to explain. "He was an immigrant with no money, and he could somehow identify with my mother's pain."

To Avi, Sophie was a tortured woman. What she desperately and unsuccessfully sought, he felt, was affection, first from her husband, later from her daughters. "Most of the people directly involved in the family were scared of her," he would say in his accented, stilted English. "She was a mean woman. By that I mean she would scream and yell and hurt people."

Debbie had warned him that her mother would judge him by the way he looked and dressed, and he had been frightened the first time they met. Yet at that first meeting he felt he saw something in her that her own daughters could not see. "Not that she wasn't mean or insulting," he explained. To Avi, Sophie had a whip and was driving everyone around her crazy. Yet to Avi, Sophie was doing this out of love. "The way she pushed her daughters was resented but it came from the heart."

Because his own mother had been poor, Avi had prided himself on never accepting money from her. But he allowed Sophie to pay for him whenever they went out to restaurants, to movies, or to the theater. And because he was not afraid of her, he did not hesitate to walk up to her and suddenly give her a hug or a kiss, or tell her he loved her, as he might to his own mother.

In Sophie, Avi had found another mother, Debbie would think. And in Avi, Sophie had found another son.

"She treated me like a son, but with one difference," Avi remembers. "She never belittled me or insulted me, as she did her own sons or her other son-in-law, Larry. I was all the things she would normally pick on, the way she picked on Larry, who didn't own a company, who just wanted to be left alone to be himself. But with me, because she knew I cared for her, she overlooked all these things."

At first when Sophie had telephoned Debbie, Debbie had been afraid to speak to her. So Avi began speaking to her instead. Sophie enjoyed their conversations. She began calling all the time. Soon she was a regular visitor.

It was Avi's warmth, Debbie felt, that for the first time in her life brought her close to her mother. One night, as the three of them were sitting in the apartment, her mother suddenly turned to her and, in that frank, direct way she had, blurted out, "Debbie, I'm so happy we can be friends now. Now I don't have to treat you as a child anymore."

Another night the three of them had been going through Debbie and Avi's wedding pictures. In one of them the sons-in-law had posed standing with Friedgood, her husband, their father-in-law, in their tuxedos. "What's similar about all these men?" Sophie asked Debbie and Avi.

Avi and Debbie tried to guess. "They're all wearing the same clothes," said Debbie, thinking of something she felt her mother cared about. "They're all wearing the same cuff links," said Avi.

But Sophie shook her head. Then she said something Debbie never forgot. "No," said her mother, beaming, "they all love their wives."

/ iii

But despite these words Sophie did not fully trust her sons-in-law. "She felt her parents' gifts had destroyed her own marriage," Debbie said of her mother years later, trying to defend, to absolve her mother, to ease her own guilt about what had happened. "She did not want the same thing to happen to her daughters."

Perhaps it was this that had led Sophie to refuse Toba the fifty thousand dollars from her trust fund—the money she needed to purchase a house after she had married Larry. After Debbie married, Sophie began insisting that all her daughters maintain separate bank accounts from their husbands'. Later, when Esther married, Sophie took all her wedding money and held it in a separate bank account in her own name. As for Beth, Sophie went even further.

The quietest of the four daughters, Beth had grown into a dark, intense, and very independent young woman. She had followed Toba and Esther to Syracuse and then had met and married a poor and struggling young intern named Jack Cook. Perhaps because the similarity between his situation and her own husband's seemed too close, after Beth's wedding Sophie ordered all her daughters to sign a statement saying that their mother would be the guardian of the trust-fund money until each reached the age of thirty-two.

All the daughters signed the statement—except Beth. Her husband had had difficulties all through medical school in meeting his tuition payments, and they needed the money. But there was more to it than that, her sisters all felt. As with Toba and Debbie, money was not important in itself to Beth. Rather, she valued her independence. That and her pride.

In 1973, when she turned twenty-one, Beth asked her mother again for her money. Again Sophie refused. Beth then hired her own attorney and filed suit against her mother.

/ iv

Of all the daughters only Esther—blond, petite Esther—had had a sustained relationship with her mother. Growing up, the others had all been afraid of their mother, not just the girls, but the boys as well. But Esther—the poised, confident one— was different. When her sisters had turned to Harriet Larsen, only Esther had stayed away. When her sisters had visited Harriet, Esther had asked them, "Why are you doing this? Don't you love your mother?"

Despite her affection for Avi, Sophie still felt Debbie, like Toba, had married beneath her. Though Beth's husband was a doctor, there was something about him she could not abide. As for her own two sons, they were no better than her sons-in-law. She had hoped they would become doctors, but neither had gotten into medical school. But Esther, Esther was different.

But for Esther, as for the others, there came a shattering break with her mother. In the spring of Esther's freshman year at Syracuse, Sophie discovered that her favorite daughter was having an affair with another student. Sophie flew up to Syracuse to confront her.

For an entire day she kept Esther locked in her room and shouted at and cursed her. Esther, the only one with enough confidence to stand up to her mother, crumbled. At the end of her visit Sophie gave Esther an ultimatum. Either she must marry the boy or she must leave college.

When Esther came home that June, Sophie did not let up. "Bitch! Whore!" she now shouted at her favorite daughter, using the same words about her she had used for Harriet Larsen and Toba. Debbie, on the point of leaving for a summer in Europe, tiptoed about the house and left, when the time came, with relief. For the next two months Esther was locked in the house at Kensington. When her friends came to visit, Sophie refused to allow them inside. When they telephoned she refused to allow Esther to speak to them. And when Debbie returned two months later, Esther seemed to her a different person.

In September, on her nineteenth birthday, Esther was married.

"Though Esther would never say it, I always felt she harbored lots of resentment toward my mother after that," remembers Debbie. "She used to be so fun-loving, so interested in dance, in painting, in creative things. But after her marriage she stopped all that. That summer my mother had intimidated her and made her feel so guilty. From then on she made up her mind to love her husband and become the perfect daughter."

"Why are you masking your feelings?" Debbie would write to her after her marriage. Esther would write back, "I can't read your letters. They are too painful."

It was as though a mist, a haze had covered her, which blinded her to her true feelings. Later, when it was all over, she would say of her parents' relationship—she, her mother's favorite, she, who had been the only one who had refused to see Harriet Larsen—now she would say how much her mother and her father had had in common; how much they had shared the same values; how close they had always been. "They loved each other very much. They could have had anything in life they wanted. It was just . . ."

But all that was in the future. After her marriage that September before her sophomore year of college, Esther returned to Syracuse and remained to earn her degree. Then, like her mother before her, she entered law school. But, unlike her mother, she received her degree.

Part III
THE DESCENT

12

IN 1973 A SEVEN-YEAR-OLD BOY WAS RUSHED TO Interboro Hospital for an emergency appendectomy. The surgeon on call at the hospital was Charles Friedgood, and a call was placed to him at home. He informed the hospital that he would arrive within the hour. An anesthetist then sedated the child.

An hour passed. But Friedgood did not arrive. Not until two hours later did he appear. By then, fearing the anesthesia might wear off, the anesthetist had sedated the child again. The child never woke up.

After this, Friedgood was dismissed from Interboro. A letter to Friedgood from administrator Owen Kaye dated September 12, 1973, reads: "As a result of either your unwillingness or inability to be at the hospital on time when you have cases scheduled for surgery and your failure to show up in some instances when you have scheduled your patients for surgery, I regret I have no alternative but to permanently suspend your admitting privileges to the hospital." Two months later, Friedgood was permanently suspended from the hospital staff.

In fact Friedgood had been in and out of trouble at the hospital for the previous eleven years. In March 1962 his gynecological-surgery privileges had been suspended for a year for reasons the hospital did not commit to writing. Six months later, on October 23, 1962, those privileges were restored.

The following year, in February 1963, the hospital's administrator, Arnold A. Feinstein, had warned Friedgood that "a great number of [your patient] charts were incomplete and the number is increasing." In March 1964 Friedgood had been issued a thirty-day suspension for improperly admitting patients to emergency beds.

Five years later, on October 17, 1968, Friedgood had been admonished by Drs. Stanley Schiowitz, Salvatore Pisciotto, and Martin Raskin for frequent lateness in the operating room. The doctors warned him that if he was more than fifteen minutes late, "the surgical procedure [would] be cancelled and rescheduled another day." A month later, on November 29, Friedgood had been notified by Feinstein that his emergency-bed privileges had again been suspended, for not visiting an emergency-room patient, in direct violation of the Emergency Board admission rules.

Yet two months later, on January 13, 1969, Friedgood had been appointed a member of the hospital's Medical Board. The following day he received a letter from Drs. Pisciotto, Raskin, and Lowell Davis of the hospital's Joint Liaison Committee, notifying him that "if the operating room supervisor finds it necessary to continually cancel your cases because of lateness we will be left with no alternative but to suspend your surgical privileges."

On July 6, 1971, Friedgood's gynecological-surgery privileges had been suspended once more. Again no reason was given. On June 29, 1972, Friedgood was notified by Dr. Schiowitz that his seniority privileges in the operating room were also being withdrawn, because of his frequent lateness.

On September 28 the hospital's new administrator, Owen Kaye, was called to investigate a case in which Friedgood—although suspended—had crossed out the name of the attending surgeon on a patient's chart and substituted his own name.

When Friedgood was dismissed from Interboro in 1973, the hospital did not specify the reasons. "The only thing the records show," explained its administrator, Robert Bornstein, four years later, "is that there was a problem of his not getting to the operating room on time."

Now Friedgood descended further, to Brooklyn's small, now-defunct private hospitals—Williamsburg General, Empire, Unity, dingy, tenementlike buildings in which he appeared to be the only surgeon—joining one after the other as the previous ones folded behind him. At the end he would find himself on the staff of Lefferts General Hospital and Linden General. Linden would go through bankruptcies and license suspensions before being forced to close after its Medicaid affiliation was revoked for health violations in the hospital. When it closed, the hospital owed the city $200,000 in back taxes. It also owed patients hundreds of thousands of dollars in malpractice claims, one of which was against Dr. Charles Friedgood.

But at Lefferts General, where Friedgood practiced when Linden closed, its last administrator, Seymour Reid, would defend Friedgood by citing his training as "the most prestigious training in surgery you can have." So highly did the hospital regard Friedgood that during the murder trial, Lefferts' operating room was open an hour early so Friedgood could perform an operation or two each morning before appearing in court.

/ ii

After he was dismissed from Interboro, Friedgood moved to a basement office on Crescent Street, two blocks away—a street where the small two-family houses were already giving way to vacant lots. Just a few blocks away was Sutter Avenue, which runs through the heart of Brownsville. Like Eastern Parkway, Sutter Avenue had once been the heart of a thriving Jewish community. Now, with the Jews long gone, the only traces of its past were the small synagogues that appeared every four or five blocks, abandoned now, vandalized, or with the word *iglesia*—"church"—written over a faded six-point Jewish star. Apartment buildings were now boarded up, the windows smashed, the insides gutted by fire or theft. Other buildings were razed, leaving rubble-strewn lots with yellow weeds already rising as high as cornstalks from cracks in the cement.

Yet life on Sutter Avenue went on. Poor blacks and Puerto Ricans had replaced the Jews. Amid the squalor, every couple of blocks, often on streets denuded of all other buildings, appeared a candy store, a grocery, a drugstore—and a medical center. Tiny one- and two-story structures, they had names like the Sutter Avenue Clinic, the East New York Medical Center, and the Blake Medical Center. It was there that Charles Friedgood, student of the renowned Isidor Ravdin, former surgical resident at the prestigious Mount Sinai and Maimonides hospitals, now began to practice.

The Sutter Avenue Clinic was run by a former Bostonian, a doctor named LaBreque. Inside, the clinic comprised ten to twelve bare cubicles, separated each from the other by wooden partitions, which doctors rented by the day, week, or month. To protect them from muggers, from the riffraff on the street, LaBreque hired a large, illiterate black man who stood outside the building with a baseball bat in his hand and escorted the doctors inside the clinic after they parked their cars. During the day, while the doctors saw patients inside, he guarded their cars on the street. When they left he escorted them back outside. Despite the neighborhood's squalor, LaBreque's income from the Sutter Avenue Clinic, according to a 1976 New York State audit, was over $100,000 a year.

For his cubicle Friedgood paid LaBreque $75 a month. He began appearing there twice a week.

Close by the Sutter Avenue Clinic was the Blake Medical Center, where Friedgood also began to practice. The Blake Medical Center was a one-story building with bars covering the front window and locks on the door even when the center was open. It was run by an Iranian doctor named Karimi, and it had no more amenities than the Sutter Avenue Clinic did—a small reception room with a linoleum floor and wooden folding chairs, and three treatment rooms, each bare save for an examining table, separated by wooden partitions. Like LaBreque's, Karimi's income, according to the 1976 New York State audit, was over $100,000 a year.

Here, too, Friedgood paid $75 a month, to Karimi, and began appearing at the Blake Medical Center twice a week. Sometimes he would bring his two sons, David and Stephen, both of whom he was encouraging to become doctors, who would help him examine patients. Sometimes he would bring Harriet and his mother as well.

Despite the surroundings, Friedgood worked as hard as ever. As he had done with the Hasidic Jews, he throve on his poor black and Puerto Rican patients. They, too, revered him. Later, during his trial, many of them trooped en masse to court on Long Island to demonstrate their support for him, and after he was released from prison on bail, they threw a party for him at his office with an elaborate cake on which was written WELCOME HOME CHARLIE.

And he saw himself as their savior. When, after the murder, police came to search his office, they discovered a black book in his desk. "You can't have that," he shouted at them. "I am a doctor. These are my confidential patient files." Believing he was lying, that there was something in the book he did not want them to find, the police confiscated it. Yet it was just as he had said. The book contained only the names and addresses of his patients.

At Blake he hired a new receptionist, Lilli Ruiz, a small, articulate woman with two teenage children and a mother to support. Like his other receptionists, she was a former patient of his, and—as always in such cases—he displayed great kindness toward her. As he did with his other receptionists, Friedgood offered to operate on her and her family, and she took him up on the offer. Besides performing surgery on her, he operated on her mother's varicose veins and on what he termed a "dropped bladder"; on her sister for what he said was a breast tumor; on her brother's hernia; on a niece for what he said was a thyroid tumor; on a nephew for what he said was a tumor on his elbow; on a first cousin for what he said were tumors on an ovary; and on a stepsister for what he said was a kidney infection and a hiatus hernia.

"He didn't care for money, only for yourself," Lilli Ruiz would say of him. "Black, white, Puerto Rican—it didn't matter to him. A person could come in here dying, and after seeing Charlie, immediately they'd feel better."

The first thing patients noticed about him, she remembered, was his smile. "Charlie had a smile—it made you feel like a million bucks. He was never in a bad mood. He never rushed in." He arrived in an old brown car with no MD plates, in old clothes, and usually in need of a haircut. "A patient doesn't need a haircut," he would say to Lilli. "He needs a good doctor."

To Lilli he was known simply as "Charlie." To his patients he was "Charlie Boy" or "Chief." "Hello, Chief; hey, Charlie Boy; how you doing?" they would call out to him as he arrived. He, in turn, called Lilli "the Professor."

Once, when a patient was sick and had no money for a cab to the hospital, Friedgood put her in his car and took her himself. "He was the only doctor I ever saw put a patient in his own car," Lilli recalled. "What other doctor would do that? Other doctors, you don't call them 'Doctor,' they look at you."

To his patients at the Blake Medical Center he was not only a surgeon but a master diagnostician. He would look into their eyes, take their pulse, and right away he seemed to know what was wrong with them. "That's right," patients would say when he told them. Soon they started telling him their problems. "Stop smoking," he would say to them. "Go home. Relax. Dance. Stop smoking."

Once, so the story went, a woman waited all day for him with a pain in her stomach that had been diagnosed as arthritis. Friedgood seemed to touch her stomach only with the tips of his fingers. "Lie on the table," he told her. "Do you spit blood?"

"Yes," she answered.

"You don't have arthritis," he told her. "You have a perforated ulcer."

"Patients couldn't believe it," said Lilli. They began bringing him presents. One man who went fishing each week came each Thursday to be treated and brought Friedgood a fresh fish. Often when Friedgood received these presents he would begin to cry. "The patients are so poor and they do this for me," he would say to Lilli. Other times he would say to her, "I'm not here for the money. I am here only to help my patients."

On Mondays Lilli would already be making appointments for the following Thursday. By the time Friedgood arrived the reception room was filled with patients waiting to see him. If the patients were not happy with another doctor's diagnosis that morning, they would return that afternoon when they knew Friedgood would be there. Other times they would refuse to see the other doctors at the clinic. They would wait for Friedgood. When he arrived, they would shout, "We love you, Charlie," and throw him kisses.

Usually when he came on Thursdays, he brought his mother with him. Lilli and his patients would marvel that they had never seen such a close relationship between a mother and a son. The old lady appeared to love coming to the center with him. "I was home and Charlie picked me up," she would say. "I'm so happy as long as I'm with my son."

And the patients adored her. While Friedgood treated them inside his cubicle, Chafke sat outside in the waiting room and talked to them. After each patient came out, Friedgood would call out to her, "Mama, are you okay?" Or the patient would put his arms around her and say, "Mama, do you love Charlie?"

Once, Lilli remembered, he came a little late. All the patients had left the waiting room and were standing outside looking for him. "There he comes, there he comes," they shouted as they saw his car approach. Those smoking cigarettes put them out. Then, with patients following him, he strode into the clinic like a king, the king of Blake Medical Center. To Lilli he turned and smiled. "Without me," he said, "they would die."

/ iii

Yet at the same time there were other kinds of stories about him—rumors, whispers. There was the woman on whom Friedgood had supposedly performed a hysterectomy who later became pregnant. And the woman on whose gallbladder he had also supposedly operated. When, years later, she developed symptoms of gallbladder problems, she had to be operated on a second time, and her doctor discovered that her gallbladder had never been touched. The surgeon was so appalled that he began malpractice proceedings against Friedgood.

Then there was Suzie Bren's childhood friend Alice Blum. Like Suzie, she had been married, and was now separated from her husband. Like Suzie, she had children to rear by herself. One day Alice mentioned to Suzie that she had felt a lump in her throat. The day before, she had been to her family doctor, who told her he had found nothing. But she was still anxious. Suzie suggested that Friedgood give her tests. Alice could then send the results to a specialist she knew, in New Jersey. Suzie called Linden General. She made an appointment for Alice to go right over.

"Dr. Friedgood signed me right in and I took the tests that afternoon," Alice said. "That night I slept in the hospital because Friedgood said they were going to give me more tests the next day."

But the next morning a man wearing a green surgical mask and green uniform appeared at her bed. "Come with me," he said. "Dr. Friedgood says you are scheduled for surgery this morning."

"For surgery?" shouted Alice, jumping up. "I'm not going anyplace. The only place I'm going is home." With that she got out of bed and called her ex-husband. "You've got to get me out of here!" she shouted to him. "I came for tests and they want to operate on me." Within the hour he arrived and took her home. She never saw Friedgood again.

As for the lump in her throat, "It dissolved by itself," she said. "It never came back." Later she went to New Jersey to satisfy herself by having other tests done. They were negative.

And there was Suzie Bren herself. Friedgood had operated on her for an intestinal blockage, making his incision along an old scar from previous surgery. This way, he said, she would have only one scar. Everything appeared to go well. But two days later, while recovering in the hospital, Suzie began feeling faint and dizzy, and had trouble breathing. Fearing she might have contracted pneumonia, attendants wheeled her to the X-ray room for a chest X ray. But when she stood up, Friedgood's sutures suddenly ruptured. Blood began spurting out as from a fountain. Immediately, transfusions were begun.

The hospital began trying to locate Friedgood. For the next two days, morning and night, Suzie also tried to locate him. She called his office, his answering service, and his home at all hours of the day and night. Not until three days later, when the danger had passed, did he appear. Where he had been, he never said; nor did Suzie ever ask him. But she knew, for there had been one place she hadn't called him. He had been with Harriet.

/ iv

Then there was the breast implant Friedgood performed on a twenty-two-year-old woman that led to a malpractice suit against him. Nanette Edelstein was a tall, thin woman with underdeveloped, childlike breasts. She lived with her parents in Brooklyn. She wanted to have her breasts enlarged, and her family doctor recommended Friedgood as a good surgeon. On July 31, 1970, at Linden General Hospital, he performed the first of five breast operations. The operation, known as an augmentation mammoplasty, is a relatively simple one. A breast implant, or prosthesis—a kind of small plastic cushion filled with a gel—is inserted into the breast. Only a small incision is necessary, no more than two inches, along the underside of the breast, for the implant can be compressed or squeezed through the opening, and the layers of skin behind it will open by themselves as the implant is inserted.

But breast surgery was not in Friedgood's area of expertise. Apparently not knowing what to do, he made an eight-inch incision across the diameter of each breast. He then inserted the implant.

Soon after the operation, when Nanette Edelstein looked at herself, she noticed something very strange. The breasts did not appear to have the normal shape. And one of the nipples was lower than the other. A week or two later she returned to Friedgood's office. Now, besides these problems, a puslike fluid was draining from the left breast. An infection appeared to have set in. Telling her that the implant itself was faulty, Friedgood took her across the street to Interboro Hospital and told her he would operate again. But instead of removing the implant and operating again, Friedgood merely resutured the breast, temporarily stopping the leakage.

In all, Friedgood resutured Nanette Edelstein's left

breast four times. Once, as he was suturing, a white, gellike substance began flowing out, but still Friedgood did not remove the implant. A few months later Friedgood left on vacation. Harriet was left in charge of his office. When Nanette Edelstein returned again, the infection had become so bad, the opening in her left breast had become so large, that Harriet became alarmed. Instead of resuturing, she reached in, grabbed the implant, and pulled it out. Nanette Edelstein stared at it in amazement. It looked like a breast covered with plastic made out of white Jell-O.

Finally Nanette Edelstein went to another doctor, a plastic surgeon. In his operation report, the plastic surgeon wrote, "On the right side a palpable implant was protruding in a somewhat superior position with the nipple below the eminence or prominence of the implant." In layman's language, what this means is that Friedgood had inserted the breast implants upside down.

Nanette Edelstein filed suit against Friedgood for malpractice. But because he was operating outside his field, his insurer disclaimed responsibility for him, claiming the company was liable for him only when he did thoracic surgery. With no malpractice insurance Friedgood had to pay for his own attorney—and the former gold-medal winner of Detroit's Philomathic Oratorical Society decided to defend himself.

Nanette Edelstein had retained the firm of Kramer, Dillof and Tessel, one of the largest malpractice firms in New York City. The attorney who represented her, James Duffy, had tried hundreds of cases. Yet what amazed Duffy about his adversary was how well Friedgood performed. Said Duffy, "He did a hell of a job."

At first, during the pretrial examination, Friedgood had seemed to Duffy a wild man. He hectored the opposing attorneys, once hurling his briefcase at one of them and then theatrically stalking out. Yet once the trial began, Friedgood turned into a different person. Suddenly, Duffy noted, he became the perfect gentleman. During recesses he would join Duffy in the hallway outside the courtroom and ask him about court procedures. Duffy would explain them to him. "Once he understood the procedures," said Duffy, "he did an excellent job."

One part of Friedgood's defense stood out in Duffy's recollections. The prosecution had called an expert witness, a Dr. Kaj Holmstrand, to testify about Friedgood's surgical procedures. Holmstrand outlined the techniques of the augmentation mammoplasty. He explained that Friedgood's initial incisions had been six inches too large; that the infection had developed because Friedgood had improperly inserted the implants; that instead of operating on Nanette Edelstein a second time, he had merely resutured the breast.

"What about the white, gellike substance that had begun flowing out of the implant?" Duffy asked him. That, explained Holmstrand, apparently resulted because Friedgood had accidentally nicked the prosthesis while he was suturing.

Then Friedgood began to cross-examine the doctor. After asking him a number of questions—how long he had practiced; how many breast implants he himself had performed—he suddenly said to him, "Doctor, did you ever have an implant that leaked gel?"

Holmstrand hesitated, realizing the trap he had set for himself. "Yes, I did," he admitted.

"Your Honor," said Friedgood, "I have no further questions."

"It was brilliant," said Duffy later. "Friedgood just left it like that. Like an expert."

Yet despite his cross-examination, Friedgood was in trouble from the start. At first he stuck to the story that he himself was not responsible for the poor results of the operation. Rather, he said, the Dow-Corning Company, which manufactured the implant, was responsible because the implant he had used was not properly sterilized. At the time of the first operation, he explained, he had simply removed the implant from its sealed box. Believing it to have been sterilized, he had merely inserted it into the body of Nanette Edelstein.

There was only one trouble with this story. In July 1970, the time of the first operation, Dow-Corning did not manufacture a sterilized breast implant. The implant it then manufactured had to be sterilized in the operating room. By his own admission Friedgood had not done that.

With that defense no longer workable, Friedgood switched to another. Now he claimed Nanette Edelstein had had numerous cysts in her breasts. Cysts could well explain why the implant had been a problem, he said.

But here again Friedgood was in trouble. Duffy and the attorney from Dow-Corning were not untrained in reading hospital records. Both of them were struck by how many notations on Nanette Edelstein's chart at Linden General Hospital appeared to be in different handwritings. Even those presumably written at the same time appeared to be in different-colored inks.

In a copy only a trained eye can detect these differences. But in the original, they become apparent. Ordinarily a hospital holds back a patient's original records for its own files and supplies duplicates instead. But because Linden General Hospital had by then been closed for health violations, the lawyers were able to subpoena not merely the duplicates but the originals as well.

In one place in the duplicate chart Friedgood had written that Nanette Edelstein "had small cystic underdeveloped breasts from childhood." But the original chart made it clear that the word "cystic," which came at the end of a line, had been inserted after the word "small" in a different-colored ink.

There was a similar insertion for August 1, 1970, the day after Nanette Edelstein's first operation. A nurse's note read, "Patient went to the bathroom and had a blackout and hit her chest and head against the lockers." The words "chest and," which appeared before "head," had, it turned out, been added to the original after the records had been subpoenaed.

And there was worse to come—evidence that would cast doubt on the entire record-keeping system of Linden General Hospital. A note sent to Friedgood from Dr. Herbert Okun, head of the Tissue Committee, dated October 27, 1972, was found: "Please note this patient has had three admissions re this condition. To date only the first chart has been requested by a lawyer. This is an opportunity to review and complete subsequent charts." And on January 9, 1973, Okun again wrote to Friedgood that he should "review charts and make necessary corrections and additions and correct diagnosis."

/ v

At the end of the trial, State Supreme Court Justice John A. Monteleone asked the jury a series of questions:

Did the plaintiff Nanette Edelstein prove that the implants were not properly inserted? The jury answered yes.

Did the plaintiff prove that Charles Friedgood negligently closed one or more incisions of the left breast, causing her injury? Again the jury answered yes.

Did the plaintiff prove that the incisions made by Charles Friedgood to insert the breast implants were negligently made, causing her injury? The jury answered yes for the third time.

Did Charles Friedgood replace the left-breast implant on October 15, 1970? The jury answered no.

Charles Friedgood was found guilty of malpractice, and Nanette Edelstein was awarded $65,000.

But again little notice was taken of the case. No mention of it was ever made in the newspapers. Nor did any regulatory body of the medical profession see fit to conduct its own investigation of Friedgood.

Once again he was able to continue.

13

AT HOME IN KENSINGTON THE ARGUMENTS BE-
tween Friedgood and Sophie had become virtually continuous. He did not come home for dinner. He did not call. She
prepared dinner and waited for him all evening. Sometimes
he did not return until ten or eleven o'clock. Sometimes he
did not return until after midnight. Then, when he arrived,
she would curse him and shout at him, "Go to your whore!
Run to your bitch!"

Or when Friedgood and Sophie would plan to meet at a
restaurant, again he would not come on time; sometimes he
would not come until an hour or two later. Again she would sit
and wait for him at the table. Then, when he arrived, she
would make a scene—"Go to your whore! Run to your
bitch!"—raising her voice loud enough so that those at the
nearby tables looked up to watch.

The only day they spent together was Sunday, when
they went to the Old Westbury Country Club to play golf together in the afternoon. Even there Friedgood had difficulties.
Among members it was whispered he could not be trusted to
keep an honest score. Once, so the story went, a new member

found himself teamed with Friedgood in a club tournament. Throughout the match Friedgood continued to move his ball and rearrange his lie. Finally, on the last hole, needing only a two-putt to put himself and Friedgood into a tie for first place with two other members, the new member deliberately three-putted and threw the match.

Friedgood didn't confine such activity to the club grounds only. One year the club's golf champion, Robert Caplan, arranged a tournament for Old Westbury members at the Doral Hotel in Miami Beach, Florida, and about fifty couples signed up for the trip—including the Friedgoods. The tournament, one for men, another for women, was played in four-somes, each man playing in a different foursome every eighteen holes. All through the match, Caplan led, followed closely by Friedgood. But all through the match, Friedgood's partners told the same story—that he was not putting in an honest score. Finally, on the last round, Friedgood edged out Caplan for the championship, and was presented with the club trophy. Later, however, his partner informed Caplan that Friedgood had again altered his score. When they returned to Long Island, his trophy was taken from him.

Meanwhile, in the women's tournament, Sophie had ended in a tie with Caplan's wife. For Sophie, crippled as she had been by the stroke, this was truly an achievement. But there could be only one winner of the tournament, and so, to break the tie, the women had to match score cards for the last eighteen holes. Though each had the same number of strokes overall, Caplan's wife had won more holes, and was declared the winner.

Sophie was distraught. "Please," she begged Caplan that night at dinner at the hotel, "your wife has won so many tournaments. Let me win this one."

Caplan was at a loss, and then he remembered that someone from the club had won a trophy at bingo the night before. Caplan walked over to the man's table and asked if he would mind donating his trophy to Sophie. "I remember I took it and brought it over to her while she was having lunch the next day. It was a trophy in the shape of a golf ball that opens up into a wine decanter with wineglasses. When I gave it to her she was the happiest person on earth."

On those Sundays when Friedgood and Sophie went to the club, they would tee off together in the early afternoon. But increasingly on Sunday mornings Friedgood would leave the house, saying he was going to the hospital; he would be back later, he would promise, and then they would go to the club. Sophie would sit home all day waiting for him. The golf course was crowded on weekends and each golfer had an appointed tee-off time; as their time approached and he still hadn't returned, she would begin telephoning his office, telephoning his answering service, telephoning his different hospitals. Their tee-off time would pass.

Sometimes they would plan to go to the club together for Sunday-night dinner. She would be all dressed up, waiting for him to come home. She would pace the living room, looking out the window for his car. She began to drink.

/ ii

To Stephen, the younger son, who lived at home, the arguments seemed to start every Friday night when his father got home. "My father would keep my mother waiting, and then, when he arrived, he would act as though nothing had happened."

"Why are you home so late?" Sophie would begin.

"Traffic," Friedgood would answer her. Or, "I was in the operating room."

"I called the operating room. You weren't there. I called your answering service. You were gone for hours." Then the tears would start.

Usually, while his mother cried and shouted, his father

picked up the newspaper. Expressionless, emotionless, he read it silently until she calmed down. Then they would go in to dinner, and the arguments would begin again.

At their center, it seemed, was always Miller's suit against Friedgood for not honoring their buy-sell agreement. The case seemed endlessly tied up in the courts. Now Friedgood wanted to settle, to accept Miller's original offer of $400,000 for So-Char's share of the Holiday Inn. But now it was Sophie who did not want to settle, and without her consent Friedgood could do nothing. After his tax-evasion trial he had signed over his shares of So-Char to her, and by refusing to settle she could keep the case tied up in litigation for years. As they sat at dinner they argued about this, and they argued about Harriet.

Friedgood had explained to Sophie that he had kept Harriet on as his nurse only for the Miller case. She had been a witness to Miller's signing the papers, he told her. That was the reason he was so nice to her. Though Sophie was certain (she told herself) that he was telling her the truth, she sensed that, once he got his hands on the money, he might run off with Harriet. And so she held firm and wouldn't settle.

Most times, it seemed to Stephen, his parents would make up. They would finish dinner and his father would go off and quietly read his paper. Or they would have Sunday lunch together, then go off to the club. One Sunday, Stephen remembered, they were to tee off at noon. "But my father did not return until three o'clock. My mother was angry, upset, a little drunk. But after she finished shouting at him, they sat down and ate lunch, and then he said to her very calmly, as though nothing had happened, 'Why don't you change?' And they left for the club."

Still, there were other times when they would not make up, when their confrontations became frightening, so frightening that the maid, Lydia, made Stephen promise never to leave her alone with his parents. One night in the fall of 1974

Friedgood came home late. Sophie was so angry at him she locked the door of the bedroom and wouldn't let him in.

"You don't love me!" she began to scream at him from behind the closed door. "So why don't you go to your whore? Run to your bitch!" Friedgood became so angry at her he rushed up the stairs and broke down the door, knocking it right off the hinges.

Stephen was not the only one to witness the fighting. One Friday night Debbie and Avi came to celebrate the Sabbath. But again Friedgood did not appear. Instead of beginning without him, Sophie insisted they all wait, at the table, while she began calling his office, his answering service, the different hospitals. By now it was after nine P.M. Still he did not come. Still she insisted they all wait.

Finally, after ten o'clock, he arrived. She began shouting at him. Friedgood ignored her and walked upstairs to his study. Sophie followed him up the stairs, cursing at him as she walked.

Debbie ran outside and looked up through the second-floor window into her father's study. As Sophie stood outside the door shouting at him, trying to open the door, Debbie saw through the window that her father had pulled his metal file cabinet from the hallway and placed it against the door to the study so she could not open it.

Her mother's cries grew more shrill. She began to shriek. Terrified, Debbie ran upstairs. There she found her mother lying on the floor outside the door to the study, crying, her crippled leg shaking. She was shrieking over and over, "He's stealing all the money. He's stealing all the money."

Avi was as frightened as Debbie by what went on in the Friedgoods' house. "What amazed me about my father-in-law," he would say afterward, "was his tremendous capacity to absorb. My mother-in-law had no hesitation in humiliating him in front of people. And he would just sit there silently, taking it.

"But when my father-in-law did become angry, he became horribly angry. One night he became so angry I thought he would kill my mother-in-law on the spot." Friedgood had returned home from work, Avi recalled, and was reading his newspaper. "I want to talk to you," Sophie said to him, and pulled down his newspaper. He tried to ignore her. Sophie began to shout at him. Suddenly he looked up at her and started to shriek, "Die! Die! Die! Why don't you die?"

/ iii

And so she drank. A martini or two at lunch. A glass of Soave Bolla or Almaden before dinner. Not that she was a lush or had "a problem," remembered her friend Renee Goodman, who lived in the wealthy Five Towns area, on the South Shore, and whom Sophie saw regularly in the last year of her life. But her drinking so terribly irritated Friedgood. Never thin, she now put on more weight. Her back began to bother her. She developed pains in her neck. She began to keep to herself. To hide her own money, she opened bank accounts and safe-deposit boxes in her own or her mother's name. Nights she took to staying up late, watching television till all hours of the morning, then sleeping late the next day, leaving notes for Lydia, the maid, not to wake her up before noon.

The house at 47 Beverly Road was neglected. Paint and plaster were peeling. The carpet was torn. Broken fixtures were not repaired. Cartons lay piled in the hallways. Books and boxes were strewn over the floors. In the bedroom sat cardboard boxes filled with business files. Next to the bed, clothes were hung on a metal laundry rack. The molding Friedgood had shattered when he tore the bedroom door off its hinges was never replaced.

Increasingly estranged from her husband, alienated, she felt, from her now-grown children, alone and friendless in Kensington, Sophie began—as much as she could with anyone—to confide in Renee. And Renee—tall and stylish, with a doting husband and two grown daughters—became her closest, indeed her only friend.

Renee returned the friendship. There was a directness, an honesty, a generosity that Renee admired in Sophie. Yet there was a hardness, a defensiveness, Renee sensed, as well. "I loved Sophie," she said of her later. "She was a brassy, batty, tough-assed broad, but I loved her."

It was as though, as Renee put it, "she was afraid to show kindness. She so wanted to be kind and giving, to do good things for people. Yet she seemed so suspicious, so afraid that in being kind, someone would be taking something from her."

Sophie had taken a liking to one of Renee's daughters, and—as she had done with her own—was forever encouraging her to go to law school. But the girl had artistic leanings and law school didn't appeal to her; instead she opened a boutique in New York City. To help her get started Sophie insisted she and Renee go to the store, where Sophie wanted to buy three baby quilts priced at two hundred fifty dollars each. But Sophie fought and haggled, so that the girl finally sold them to her for a hundred fifty dollars each. Later she jokingly told her mother never to bring Sophie to the store again.

As for her own children, Sophie never stopped complaining about them. They were all disappointments. Only of Esther did she speak with affection. Esther had become the lawyer Sophie wished she herself had been. To Sophie, Esther was the nucleus of the family. Only Esther could keep the family together. The others, she felt, had all married beneath them. Toba's husband, Larry, she described as "the beer-drinking hippie." Avi, despite his affection for her, she referred to disparagingly as "the penniless photographer."

Even Beth's husband, Jack Cook, the doctor, she did not care for. She did not trust him. Beth's lawsuit—imagine, thought Sophie, being sued by your own daughter—was in-

creasingly disturbing to her. At first there had been polite exchanges between her attorney and Beth's. She and Beth had
even made a point of telling each other the suit was "nothing
personal." Beth had even said that her mother would be the
first to understand.

But the exchanges soon turned bitter. Beth's attorney
filed an order demanding that Sophie show cause why she
should not be held in contempt of court for refusing to turn
over Beth's assets. Five times, once at eight o'clock in the
morning, a process-server appeared at 47 Beverly Road to
serve Sophie with a subpoena to appear in court. Each time he
got as far as the front door, only to be told by Lydia that Mrs.
Friedgood was not at home.

Matters grew steadily worse until February 1975, when
Beth and her husband met with Sophie and Friedgood. Because Renee's husband was an attorney, Sophie asked him and
Renee to join them. The meeting took place in Kensington, at
the house on Beverly Road, and it began amicably enough,
with everyone acting as if it were a social, rather than a legal,
gathering. But things quickly turned bitter. Finally Friedgood
begged Beth to drop her suit, and neither Renee nor her husband could forget the hate in her voice as she replied.

"I just want my money," Beth responded. "That's all I
care about. And I don't care if my mother rots in jail."

When the court finally ruled in Beth's favor, Sophie still
refused to turn over the money to Beth.

/ iv

Sophie would even speak to Renee of Harriet Larsen, trying to
joke about her in that hard way she had. She would call her
"the whore," or, in Yiddish, the *nofke.* "I know the Harriet
stories," she would say to Renee, "but they don't bother me."

But it was when she spoke of her husband that Sophie's
tone and disposition altered. True, she complained about him,

not only to Renee but to anyone else who would listen to her; about his mother, Chafke, whom she now forbade in her house; about his business dealings, which she felt he did not understand. Yet hard as she had become, when she said his name she truly seemed to melt. "My Charles," she would call him. Even his lies she somehow appeared to tolerate, even— in some strange way—to romanticize. To Renee she spoke of him as "the Magnificent Deceptor."

Because she knew Sophie loved him, Renee said to her, "Sophie, why are Harriet and Chafke always in Charles's office with him? Why do they always tell him how wonderful he is? Why don't you go to his office and tell him how wonderful he is also?"

Her reply, thought Renee, was typical of Sophie. "Because," she said, "I can't lie like they do."

She seemed unable to stop herself from speaking her mind, from telling the truth as she saw it. Once, Renee was suffering from back pain and Friedgood suggested she come with him to one of his hospitals, where he could put her in traction. "Don't let him touch you!" cried Sophie. "You don't need to go to a hospital." Then, to make light of what she had said, she added in her blunt, brassy way, "Look, you have back pain—just tuck in your stomach, pull in your ass, and take two aspirin."

Yet, despite her directness, despite her honesty, or perhaps because of it, there was a naiveté about Sophie that Renee found startling. One evening, as Renee was preparing dinner, Sophie called her. They began to talk, to gossip— "woman talk," Renee recalled. "We talked about Charlie and my husband, about what they liked, what they didn't, comparing the two, comparing notes." At the end of the conversation, she remembered, as they were about to hang up, Sophie said to her, almost—it seemed—as an afterthought, "Renee, did your husband ever say he would murder you?"

/ v

Yet Sophie continued to believe that someday, somehow it would all work out between her and her husband. No matter how much he was in debt, no matter how badly he managed his money, even if they lost the Miller case, her own money would get them through. She purchased a condominium near Palm Beach in Florida, and it became her home away from home, her dream house. It was there, she said, she hoped to move with Charles, away from New York, away from Kensington, away from Harriet, to a new place, a new home, where they could begin a new life, where the two of them would live happy and alone.

Renee, who had a winter home in Aventura, just an hour away, became her decorator. What Sophie wanted, Renee remembered, was to design the house so that there would be enough beds in it for her six children and their husbands or wives to stay. "They're going to come," she would say to Renee happily. "They got to sleep, don't they?"

What Renee also remembered was that Sophie wanted two desks for the living room—one for her, the other for Charles, so that he couldn't shut her out. "I remember her in every store making every male salesman about Charles's size sit down in it to make sure his desk chair would be the right size."

So they traveled back and forth to New York to buy. And they flew back and forth to Florida to design. And yet to Renee it was becoming clear it was all somehow too late. She remembered how at night, when the two women were in Florida, Sophie would call home to talk to her husband, and that she would then call his office and his answering service and the hospitals, but he was never there. And that while she was there he would never, ever call her.

And she remembered another day, a day back on Long Island, not long before the end, when she and her husband had been together with Sophie and Charles at the Old Westbury Country Club. They were to have played golf that day, the four of them, and her husband had taken the day off from work. But, as usual, Charles did not show up on time, so they played the first nine holes without him. Then, when he arrived, they all decided to stay and have dinner at the club. It was a buffet, Renee remembered. When Sophie and Renee's husband went to get food, she and Charles stayed at the table. Watching Sophie gathering up food at the buffet table, Charles leaned over to her and said, "Look at her, Renee. Look at my wife. She looks like a fat pig."

And later, after Sophie died, Renee remembered yet another night. They were in a Chinese restaurant in the Five Towns area, she, her husband, and Friedgood. When her husband stepped away, she and Friedgood began to talk. "You know, Charles," she began, "I loved Sophie."

"So did I," he answered. "I loved her, too."

"But all the fighting, Charles, all the fights you had with her . . ."

"What fights?" she remembered his saying to her. "We got on so well together."

14

IN 1974 HARRIET BECAME PREGNANT AGAIN. THIS time she made no attempt to hide it. She seemed very proud, her friends remembered, and there was no question of who the father was.

Again she returned to Denmark to have the baby. After she had left, Friedgood told Sophie he had to go to a medical convention in Arizona; but instead, despite the fact that the terms of his probation on the income-tax conviction forbade him to leave the country, he flew to Denmark to join Harriet. In the fall of 1974 Harriet gave birth to a little girl. They named her Matte—in Hebrew they called her Rachel.

As before, when Harriet returned to the United States there was a question about where she would stay. Now there were two children, instead of just one, and a Danish girl to help care for them. Sophie was away in Florida when Harriet returned, and the house in Kensington was empty. So for the first two weeks, Harriet, the two children, and the Danish maid stayed there.

They could, of course, remain only until Sophie returned. By then Friedgood had located an unfurnished apartment for them in Douglaston, in Queens, not far from her former one in Bayside. To furnish it, he brought items from the house on Beverly Road—things that Sophie later thought she had lost—Sophie's old portable television, a quilt she thought she had misplaced.

Now Harriet was borrowing not only Sophie's husband but her possessions, and she began to want something of her own. She started insisting that Charles leave Sophie. But Friedgood appeared reluctant to do this while the Miller case was still in litigation. Just as he had told Sophie that he needed Harriet for the Miller case, he now said the same thing about Sophie to Harriet.

He explained to Harriet that all his money, nearly a million dollars, was tied up in the Miller case. Because of Miller, he said, he had signed over all his assets to Sophie. That way, he explained, if he declared bankruptcy, Miller could not touch any of it. More important, he told Harriet, he needed Sophie to testify for him at the trial. Sophie, he told her, had been a witness when Miller signed papers that turned over much of the money to him.

After the trial was over, after everything was settled, he would convince Sophie to sign over all his assets back to him. Then, he promised Harriet, he would tell Sophie the truth about them and the two children, and would ask her for a divorce. They would move away from New York, the two of them and the babies, even leave the United States. They might settle in Denmark, he said, where she could have her own home and a car. Or perhaps in Israel if Denmark did not work out. He urged her to be patient until then. Sophie, he reminded her, was a crazy woman. She was, he said, capable of anything.

To her friends Harriet now complained more than ever of "crazy Sophie." When her friends asked her what was happening—why Friedgood hadn't left Sophie, why he hadn't asked for a divorce, how long she was supposed to wait—she would say to them, "Only the Miller case is keeping us apart."

Yet her friends were not so sure. Seeing how Friedgood

lived; the old clothes he wore; the old Cadillac he drove; seeing how Harriet's apartment in Douglaston lacked furniture, even curtains, they wondered whether it was really money that was keeping him from leaving his wife. Harriet, her friend Lena felt, was living "in a fairyland, a fantasy world. She would talk about how Friedgood's children loved her and called her 'Mama' and how they hated Sophie. She talked of Friedgood's kids—Sophie's kids—as being her own, of being within the same family structure. She would say she had eight children and soon would have grandchildren as well. Even Friedgood's mother she referred to as her mother-in-law."

On Christmas Eve, 1974, Friedgood and Harriet visited the Pingels. With them they brought the two babies, and Ole Pingel later remembered how happy Friedgood seemed then with Harriet and the children. Gone were his earlier objections to Harriet's celebrating Christmas; now he accepted it. And he bathed and fed and changed the babies, proudly referring to Heinrich as "my son."

Later, talking about the children to Pingel, he said, "I have six of my own."

"No, eight," Harriet corrected him. "You have eight of your own."

It was about this time that Friedgood began asking Pingel questions about Denmark. He had been to Denmark, he told Pingel. He liked the people very much. His wife was crazy, mentally sick, he would explain; then he would say he wanted to live either in Denmark or on a *kibbutz* in Israel. He never said directly he would leave Sophie. Instead he asked how hard it would be for a doctor to find work in Denmark; if jobs were available where one could live; what kind of car a doctor should drive; if he should bring his Cadillac or buy a Volvo; what kinds of investments, stocks or bonds, could bring him the greatest return.

But although he was Harriet's friend, Pingel found himself discouraging Friedgood from moving to Denmark. His brother was a doctor, and he would tell Friedgood how difficult it was to get work there. Lena would also discourage Harriet from moving to Denmark with Friedgood. "Why don't you stay and work here?" she would say to her. "He is an old man and you are asking him to go to a country where he doesn't even speak the language. Here he has prestige. There he will be a nobody."

Harriet appeared in a quandary. Living in Douglaston with her two children and the maid, with little furniture, no curtains, not even a carpet, she began having periods of despondency. When Lena visited her she was startled to hear Harriet say, "How I envy you. I am so sick and tired of living like this. I am living in a suitcase, on other people's stuff. I don't even have any furniture. I want a normal family."

"She began," said Lena, "telling me how lucky I was."

But there was something else, Lena noticed, about Harriet she had never seen before. She was afraid. "I remember one time she was especially upset. She was waiting for Friedgood to call. She had done some decorating and bought wall-to-wall carpeting, but she said it didn't matter. She began saying it didn't matter where they went, Sophie would come and get them. She would send people after them to kill her and the children." Lena didn't understand.

/ ii

For Avi and Debbie, Harriet had become a growing source of concern. Though Avi had visited her with Debbie in the early days of their marriage, before he came to know Sophie, he was now increasingly disturbed by the relationship, by his own involvement. Not only because he cared so for his mother-in-law but because his father-in-law had never admitted, had never acknowledged to him and Debbie, just what his relationship with Harriet was. Out of Harriet's presence he called her "the nurse," never Harriet. Nor would he admit to them even that

Heinrich was his son. Of course—listening to him talk proudly of the boy, watching him at Harriet's apartment throwing the baby up in the air, then holding him upside down by his feet as he did—it was difficult not to realize. Heinrich himself called Friedgood "Papa." He resembled Debbie's older brother David. And he was named after their grandfather. . . .

Late at night, sitting in the living room of their apartment in the East Village, he and Debbie tried to make sense of it. Did her father really love Harriet? If so, where did that leave her mother? And what were they to do? Were they to continue to see Harriet and not tell Sophie? Wasn't their first obligation to her, whom they both loved?

Debbie had at this time begun working as a secretary to a Yiddish writer. He was an old man, in his seventies, though he was writing as prolifically as ever. Gentle and humble, short and slight, his bald head as white as a Ping-Pong ball, he had an almost saintly appearance. He had been born in Eastern Europe into a Hasidic family, most of whom had been murdered by the Nazis. He had managed to escape to America. But though he was alive, Yiddish, the language in which he wrote, was dying. It was hard for him to find an audience for his writing. Speaking no English, for years he had lived in furnished rooms and eaten in cafeterias. For years his stories—of ancient Hasidic myths, of mysticism, of the supernatural, of superstition—had barely sold.

Something about him, about his life, about his writing, had attracted Debbie to him. His characters—the poor, suffering old men in full beards and long black coats who spoke only Yiddish—had been her father's patients in Brooklyn when she was a little girl. The themes of his stories were evil, guilt, and betrayal—and these same feelings she now felt for herself. She felt she was entangled in her father's web, that she was unable to free herself and tell her mother the truth. The same devils and demons that tore at the souls of the Jewish writer's tormented characters were, she sensed, tearing at her own soul.

Years later, when it was all over, the writer would listen to her for hours in his apartment as she poured out her grief and her guilt. The nightmares had begun for her. Each night it was the same. She awakens in her apartment in the middle of the night. Everything is black. She is alone. Outside in the hallway, on the narrow, dimly lit stairway, stands her father. In his hand is a needle. He is waiting for her, waiting to kill her. She begins to scream. But she is unable to utter a sound.

The old man would sit and listen to her as she told him these dreams. "Sometimes," he would say to her as she described all she had done in those troubled days, "in cases like yours, it is better to do nothing. Would what you did have made any difference to your mother? Would it have helped? No, the only difference is that your father would now be free."

/ iii

At the time, the answer had seemed so simple, so straightforward to her. As Avi had said to her, it was simply a matter of "honesty," of "integrity," not only for Sophie's sake but for her own. The solution, he had said, was to confront her father.

So Debbie had attempted to do so. First she approached Harriet. But Harriet would not talk to her. "I can't tell you anything," she said to her. "I am not allowed to."

All Harriet would tell her was, "Your father is a wonderful man."

At Avi's urging she now tried to talk to her father, to get him to admit the extent of his relationship with Harriet. But when she spoke to him, he denied everything. "What? What?" he said to her. "What are you trying to say to me?" As he had told Sophie, he now told Debbie he needed Harriet simply to testify in the Miller case. There was nothing more to their relationship.

"He was so believable," says Debbie. "He explained it all so well. And I wasn't strong enough to pursue it."

Now Avi began to call him. He and Debbie began leaving messages with his answering service. "Come to us to eliminate the rumors," they would say into the phone. But he would not return the calls. Finally Avi persuaded Debbie to leave the following message: "Papa," said Debbie, "if you don't come to us to discuss the rumors, it will be your loss, because we are going to tell Mommy all we know. And we don't take responsibility for what will happen." It was only then that he agreed to meet with them.

In the summer of 1974, with Harriet in a late stage of her second pregnancy, he came to their apartment. Unexpectedly he brought Harriet. It was a hot night, and Harriet, Avi remembered, was out of breath from climbing six flights of stairs. They all sat down in the small living room. Despite Harriet's presence, Avi began to question his father-in-law.

"I really don't like the rumors going around the family," he began nervously, in his stilted way of speaking. "I would like to know now. We would like to know what is going on. We have affection for you, and it would help us a lot if you told us directly what is the relationship between you and Harriet."

With that, Harriet began to speak. "Not now," his father-in-law said, stopping her and placing his hand atop hers. He smiled at her, then at Avi and Debbie. "We have many things to think about," he began. "We all have problems. Especially you," he said, looking at Debbie and Avi. "You have to think of your own future and not get caught up in other things that are happening, because there really isn't that much to worry about."

"But, Papa," Debbie persisted, "there are so many rumors going around about Harriet. Nobody knows any details. We're begging you to lay it on the line. If you love Harriet, why don't you get a divorce, Papa? Why don't you leave Mommy?"

"I have to make Mommy happy," he answered her. "I have to wait for the Miller case to be over. All I need now is a divorce. Miller would love that."

"But do you plan to leave Mommy after the Miller case is over?" she heard herself saying. Without speaking, her father nodded.

"Then where will you go? What will you do?"

"Maybe Harriet and I will go to Israel," he answered softly. Then, in his strange way of justifying himself, he added, "If I go there, I will educate Heinrich in a *yeshiva*."

Shortly afterward Friedgood and Harriet stood up to leave. As they began walking down the narrow staircase Avi stopped him. "Chuck," said Avi, who was so devoted to Sophie, who thought of her as he would his own mother, "what is it you see in her? What does she have that Sophie doesn't?"

Without turning, without looking at him, his father-in-law said, half out loud, half to himself—the first and only time Avi had heard him speak candidly about Harriet—"She gives me warmth." He then looked up at Avi. He smiled. "You come from Egypt. You know. Muslims have two wives, don't they?"

Avi resolved never to see Harriet again.

/ iv

Harriet stayed in America only two months after she returned with her second child. In March 1975 she abruptly left for Denmark. Whether Friedgood had frightened her with more stories of "crazy Sophie"; whether, as she told her friends, Chafke had told Sophie about her because Harriet had replaced her in her son's affections—Harriet felt she was being followed, that she and her children were being watched. Once she told Inge Pingel she had seen Sophie and Stephen pull up to the apartment building in a car. Stephen had walked up to the building and peered through her blinds.

Another time, said Inge, "she called me up hysterically. 'Somebody is watching the house,' she cried. 'Strangers are watching my children.'" She claimed she had seen a car drive slowly by as if watching the building. Other times she said she saw a man sitting outside in a car taking pictures.

She could not sleep nights. She would have her friends sleep over or she would keep the lights on all night. "I look out the window and someone is there all the time," she would say. Once, when Ole Pingel visited her, she was afraid to open the door for him. She told him she was afraid someone would kidnap her children.

/ v

One weekend morning that spring, when Avi and Debbie were spending the night in Kensington, her father came downstairs to their bedroom at eight o'clock. "Harriet is leaving today for Denmark," he announced. "Would you like to see her before she goes?"

It had been nine months since they had seen her—the last time had been that summer evening before she had had her baby. "No," Debbie said, "I don't want—"

"It's her last day in the United States," said her father. "Your mother is still asleep. We have a luncheon at the club at noon. If we leave now, we can be back before she wakes up."

It was Avi who decided for her. "If he really wants us to, then we'll say good-bye."

Friedgood drove them to Douglaston. "When we arrived," Avi remembered, "there was barely any furniture in the house—just a baby in the cradle and about ten suitcases on the floor." They saw Heinrich come up to Friedgood and begin hugging him. He had changed in the past months, they noticed. He had grown. "He hugged my father," said Debbie, "and called to him, 'Papa, Papa.' "

Harriet, they both noticed, had been crying; now she wandered from room to room, distractedly packing. It was then Debbie noticed her mother's quilt, the small television set she had been looking for, and some of her old luggage.

Harriet led Friedgood into the kitchen. "Are you going

to stay more than ten minutes this time?" they heard her whisper to him. Minutes later she reappeared to speak to Avi and Debbie. She couldn't stand it anymore, she said. She told them how Stephen and Sophie had been outside the building, that Stephen had come up and peered in through the blinds. She told them that a strange car had been following them. Then suddenly she began to cry. "I don't think I can manage alone," she sobbed. "I am afraid of airplanes."

It was pitiful, Avi thought. She had all this luggage and the two babies. On the spur of the moment, an idea came to him. He had nothing against Harriet. She had never done him any wrong. So, to help her with the luggage, he made a suggestion to his father-in-law. If Friedgood would pay, he, Avi, would fly over on the plane to Denmark with Harriet. He could stay overnight and return the next day.

Harriet seemed to like the idea. His father-in-law seemed to also. As they left he told Harriet he would drive Debbie and Avi back to Kensington and return with Avi to take her to the airport that night. But when they were in the car driving back to Kensington, his father-in-law turned to him. "It won't be necessary for you to go with her," he told him. "She can go by herself."

"And when we returned to Kensington he changed out of his clothes into a suit for the club. Before my own eyes I saw him transform himself. Just as he had deceived Sophie all those years, I saw now he was deceiving Harriet," Avi said.

The following week he persuaded Debbie to tell her mother the truth.

/ vi

The following weekend they again slept over at Kensington. Late Friday night, after his father-in-law had gone to bed, Avi and Debbie sat up in the living room with her mother until three A.M.

"We told her everything," said Avi.

For Avi the matter was still simple and straightforward. Years later, in describing his motives, he would again use the words "honesty" and "integrity." Debbie's feelings were far more complex. Years later she would remember the clothes her mother was wearing as she sat on the couch facing them, how her head was tilted in that special way she had as she listened, impassive. Yet, as she poured out the stories about her father, at the same time Debbie sensed something telling her to stop.

"I felt guilt. I felt I was betraying my father. A year before, my loyalty had been to him. I had loved Harriet. Before, if my mother had asked me, I would have told her nothing. But now I was changing about my mother and my father. I felt she trusted us as friends and that I was talking to her for the first time as woman to woman."

And so she told her. With Avi prodding her, she told her mother of visits to Harriet, of the letters she had written her, of her own friendship with Harriet over the years. She explained that the child Heinrich, whom she had seen just the week before, now called her father Papa, that his curly blond hair and face resembled David's; but that when they had tried to confront her father he had refused to admit that Heinrich was his son. Finally they told her about the conversation they had had with him at their apartment last June, how he had told them, in front of Harriet, that all his money was tied up in the Miller case, that he needed Sophie as a witness, and that he intended to leave her when the case was over.

"You sound very convincing," her mother said to her when at last Debbie had finished and her mother started up the stairs to bed. "If it's true, it's a pity. But I would still rather believe your father."

But the next morning Sophie awoke earlier than Debbie remembered she had done in years. At eight A.M. she entered Avi and Debbie's bedroom with Friedgood beside her. "Charles," she said, "look Avi in the eye and swear to him you have had no relationship with Harriet."

"I swear," said Friedgood, looking straight ahead, away from them.

"Now swear on your mother's life you have had no relationship."

"I swear," he said again.

Then, without a word, he turned and walked out of the bedroom. "Where are you going?" Sophie cried out. "When are you coming back?" But he didn't answer.

15

WITH HARRIET GONE, SOPHIE MADE A NEW EFFORT.
She lost weight. She went to the beauty parlor to have her hair
styled and frosted. She began taking an interest in Friedgood's
office in Brooklyn on Crescent Street. She met Blackie and Suzie Bren. She learned how to fill out her husband's medical
forms. She talked about decorating the office. Once, at the end
of the day, Suzie Bren happened to notice Friedgood and Sophie walking together from the office out to their car. They
were holding hands.

    And that was how she finally crossed the path of Harri-
et's friend Ole Pingel. He had planned a trip back to Denmark, but had been forced to change his flight plans because
of illness in the family; now, to obtain a refund, he needed a
doctor's signature. So on the morning before he was to leave,
Pingel arrived at Friedgood's office in Brooklyn, and Sophie
was there. Sophie noticed him immediately—he was tall, nearly six feet, thin and attractive, with Nordic features. He stood
out from Friedgood's regular black and Hispanic patients. "I
don't know you," she said. She began to chat with him.

    "Are you married? Do you have children? How long
have you been in America?" she wanted to know. She ap-

peared genuinely interested, Pingel felt. He warmed to her immediately.

"Would you like to take me to lunch?" Sophie suddenly asked him.

"No, I'm sorry, I can't," he said, explaining he had only come for her husband's signature so he could catch a plane later that day. Instead he suggested that when he returned they all have dinner together. "I was surprised," he said afterward, "because she was so nice, so pleasant, and all that I had known from Harriet for six years was how crazy 'crazy Sophie' was. But here was a nice, intelligent woman. What goes on here? I thought."

/ ii

Very late one evening after Harriet had gone, Debbie, in her apartment in the East Village, received a phone call from her mother. She was crying. She was hysterical. But when Debbie asked what was wrong she hung up.

A few minutes later she called again. "He's beating me. He's going to kill me," Sophie kept repeating. "This has been going on for six years. I'm so unhappy. Help me. Help me. Talk to me." Terrified, Debbie dialed the Kensington police.

Alone in the police booth on Beverly Road at the edge of Kensington Village, Raymond Sickles, the chief of Kensington's six-man police force, took the call. A hulk of a man, with gray-white hair, a huge chest and belly, Sickles insisted on wearing a white shirt and tie as part of his police uniform. Sickles could move quickly when he had to. And on this warm spring night, after he spoke to Debbie, he got into the station wagon parked outside the booth, drove a few blocks to 47 Beverly Road, walked up to the front door, and rang the bell.

A few minutes past midnight Debbie received another call from her mother. "Debbie, Debbie," Sophie cried, "I can't believe you called the police."

"And the next day," Debbie remembered, "she was in

such a good mood. She said to me, 'I think your father is a big idiot. I think Harriet is trying to blackmail him over the Miller case. You kids are so stupid. You don't know anything. He couldn't possibly have two women.' "

/ iii

But now, in the afternoons, when the house was empty except for the maid, Lydia, Sophie began searching for a clue, rummaging about in her husband's belongings—his clothes, his closets, his desk drawers. One afternoon she came upon his passport in a pocket of one of his jackets hanging in a closet. Opening it, she saw that in the past year he had been to Denmark. Leafing through the pages, she discovered, folded between them, the pictures of Harriet and of a blond, curly-haired boy—and the letters.

March 11

MY LOVE,

If you only knew how much I love you ... you would forget about everything else ... hurry—I need you now, love you, miss you so much, but I will not wait anymore.

And another.

April 15

We can't live without Papa, and we don't want all the money. We want him. ... The least we could do is to be together.

And still another.

May 1

... Think of what you want to sacrifice, some of the money or us! Oh sweetheart, I mean it, so serious; so do something now, please.

/ iv

"What do you want to do—call the police?" said Renee Goodman when Sophie called to tell her what she had found. "They'd take him to jail for violating his probation." Instead, Renee told Sophie to hide the passport away in a safe place where no one could find it. The following day Sophie put the passport, along with the letters and the pictures, into one of the safe-deposit boxes that she had recently opened to keep her stocks, bonds, and jewelry, a place where only she and her mother could get at them. She also did one other thing Renee suggested. She hired a private detective.

Still, as she had done with her own daughters, Sophie drew lines about herself that she would not permit Renee to cross. When Sophie's mother came to visit her in Kensington, Renee drove over to meet her. When Sophie left the room the old lady began speaking to Renee. "You know about Sophie and Charles?" she began. "You know the troubles—" Suddenly Sophie reentered the room. She spoke sharply to her mother in Yiddish. Though Renee did not speak Yiddish, she understood it. "Shut up!" she understood Sophie to say to her mother. Then, pointing to Renee, Sophie added, "She doesn't know anything."

How painful it was for her she could never let Renee or anyone else know. Though she had told Renee of finding the passport with the letters and the pictures of Harriet and the baby, there was something about the picture of Harriet she had not, she could not, bring herself to tell Renee. In the picture Harriet was nude.

/ v

And yet . . . And yet she refused to give up hope. She reread the letters. Rereading them, she began to see them in a different light, sensing something in them she had not before.

Mar 31

My love, I feel bad very much about my reaction the last few months in N.Y. I think everything was too much for me, and I think also for you.... Why am I back here and you there? ... I am so worried.

and

You promised me you would call me often.... What did you say? You promised me once a week or once every other week. And [it] isn't that expensive, please let me hear your voice, at least. I can't stand this here. I don't know what to do.... I am ... taking deep breaths so I just should not cry.

And finally,

I don't know how to impress on you, that if you want us really, you will have to be here soon ... she is just sitting back like a witch laughing, I know that she got you in her hands.... I will not be in this miserable situation any more, having the man I love being with another woman in the same house, have to take her out to dinners, weddings, and much more. I don't want any other father for my children but I have to live and so do they.

/ vi

Final papers in the Miller case went before Nassau County Judge Daniel G. Albert in April. At issue was the price Miller was required to pay Friedgood for his share of the Holiday Inn—the $400,000 Miller had originally offered or the $1 million that the share was reportedly worth. On June 9 Friedgood's attorney received a letter from the judge's law clerk saying a decision in the case was imminent. On Friedgood's instructions the attorney began calling the judge's clerk every other day.

At the beginning of June a cousin of Friedgood's arrived in America from Israel. His name was Sholem Cohen. He was a cantor who had come to find work for the High Holidays. Friedgood invited him to stay at 47 Beverly Road.

He was a tall, well-built man, ruddy-complexioned, with a full head of white hair, a powerful voice, and a heavy Yiddish accent. To find work for him, Friedgood had taken him to some of the synagogues he knew in Brooklyn. But as Cohen said later, "They had not been the kind of synagogues I expected from someone in such a large house." Sholem Cohen had been surprised.

Sholem Cohen was further surprised at how frequently his cousin stayed away from home. Even Friday nights, when Sophie waited for him to celebrate *Shabbos,* which meant so much to her, he was not there. "She was there with her kerchief, with the candles," Sholem Cohen would remember. "She wanted everything to be right. Then, when he finally came home, he would sit there reading the paper, and they would have terrible, terrible fights."

Though in the weeks he had stayed in Kensington he had never gotten to know his cousin, he had come to know Sophie. In the morning, after she awoke—she started to awaken earlier since he was there—they would sit together and talk while the maid, Lydia, served them breakfast. Like Ole Pingel a stranger, Sholem Cohen, too, sensed Sophie's warmth and genuine concern about him. Though she hardly knew him, he felt she had taken him into her confidence. She spoke to him of her children—of her daughter who had married the hippie; of the one who had married the penniless photographer; of her third, who was suing her own mother. In fact, he would remember later, she would tell him about everything, everything but herself and her husband.

/ vii

Ole Pingel had gone to Denmark at the end of May, and three weeks later, on June 15, just before returning to America, he telephoned Harriet. He remembered her first words to him were about Sophie.

"I heard you spoke to crazy Sophie," Harriet began.

"Yes," he answered, "she was very nice."

"Did she talk about me?"

"No, she didn't."

"Well, it doesn't matter now. Everything is taken care of. He is coming soon."

"I've heard that one before."

"It's just a very, very short time. I can now see the end to our being separated."

/ viii

On Tuesday, June 17, 1975, Sophie Friedgood left her house at eight A.M. She was playing in the semifinals of a golf tournament at Old Westbury. Later that evening she was to meet her husband for dinner at Lundy's restaurant in Brooklyn, a favorite of theirs, off the Belt Parkway at Sheepshead Bay. From there they were to go to their accountant, a tax specialist, to discuss the nearly $400,000 Friedgood still owed the government. If it were not then too late, they planned to drive on to the South Shore and visit Renee and her husband.

Sophie's partner in the tournament was the wife of an attorney. She had not known Sophie before the tournament but she would remember how encouraging Sophie had been in their earlier matches. That Tuesday she and Sophie won their semifinal match, and Sophie was ecstatic.

At four-thirty that afternoon, still excited about her own and her partner's victory, Sophie went to the club's golf shop and ordered a new golf bag for her husband. "He's conservative," she told the golf pro, explaining she wanted a black bag for him. She then picked out a new bright-yellow bag for herself.

At six P.M. she arrived at Lundy's. As Friedgood was not yet there, she sat down at a table by herself and ordered a bottle of wine. When the waiter brought it, she began chatting with him, asking him about himself, his family, his job. "I was attracted to the lady," the waiter would later say. "She was very nice." The waiter also remembered Friedgood, who arrived, in his own car, an hour later. "Because of the lady I expected something from the man. He didn't even leave me a tip."

At eight P.M. Sophie looked at her watch. "Charles," she said. They stood up and walked outside to the parking lot, then separately drove to their accountant's house in their two cars.

When they arrived at eight-thirty, the accountant remembered, both Sophie and Friedgood appeared in good spirits. The accountant offered Sophie a drink, but she took only a glass of water. As they discussed their financial situation with him, Sophie began kidding him, asking whether he would be able to get them a tax refund for the years 1962 to 1964. That would help settle things, she said.

They stayed at the accountant's for an hour. Before leaving, at nine-thirty, Sophie telephoned Renee. They were just going, she said; they would be at Renee's within the hour.

But they did not go to Renee's. Instead—without ever calling her back—they returned, each in a separate car, to Kensington. Nobody was home. Lydia had left for the night. Sholem Cohen had gone to the city to stay overnight with a cantor friend who was helping him look for work.

Then, at eleven o'clock, the telephone rang. Friedgood answered it. It was Esther. She and her husband, both of whom had just been graduated from law school, were visiting his parents in New Jersey. The next day they were planning to drive to Kensington, and they wanted to know when they should arrive. "We called before, but you weren't home," she said.

Friedgood said he and Sophie had been out and had just arrived home from dinner. Then Sophie got on. "I was playing golf all day, in a tournament. My golf partner's husband is an attorney. Which reminds me—why don't you speak to him about a job tomorrow, when you come home?"

Six minutes later, Esther hung up. Friedgood and Sophie walked upstairs and undressed for bed. Then—as the medical examiner later reconstructed it—Friedgood went to the file cabinet in his study. There, in the top drawer, was a long needle and syringe. While Sophie waited for him to come to bed, he filled the syringe with the painkilling drug Demerol.

Without speaking he walked back to the bedroom. Sophie lay on her back, waiting for him to lie down beside her. Suddenly he grabbed her arms, stretched them above her head, and injected the contents of the syringe up under her armpit.

It was a strong dose, strong enough to knock her out, though not enough to kill her. And it would be perhaps ten, fifteen minutes before the drug started to take effect.

Sophie began to scream. But nobody was in the house to hear her. She began to kick, to fight. But nobody was in the house to help her. With both hands Friedgood turned her over and held her facedown on the bed, on her stomach, pinning her arms behind her so she couldn't strike him, so she couldn't scratch him, so she couldn't fight back as he waited for the drug to take effect.

Within minutes she began to feel drowsy. Friedgood loosened his grip. She lay there on the bed, eyes open, motionless. He took the needle and jabbed it up under the other armpit. Once, twice, a third time, in her armpit, in her thigh, in her buttocks.

Still she was breathing. She lay on her stomach, silent, moribund, but still alive, as though refusing to die. Friedgood watched her with growing impatience. Finally he turned her over, onto her left side, and for the last time, he put the needle up into the right side of her chest, plunging it between her ribs, all the way into her liver.

Moments later her breathing stopped. He took the needle and syringe, and returned them to the top drawer of the file cabinet across the hallway. Then he walked back to the bedroom, lay down beside his wife, and went to sleep.

16

THE WEDNESDAY MORNING COMMUTER TRAFFIC
was already building on the Long Island Expressway when,
shortly before seven-thirty A.M., Lydia Fernandez, driving out
from the city against the traffic, turned her car off the expressway at exit 33, just over the Nassau County line, and headed
north toward Kensington. Lydia was more than just a housekeeper for the Friedgoods. Since coming to the United States
ten years before from the Dominican Republic, she had been
until the past year their live-in maid, and regarded herself, in
her own words, "as one of the family."

"Mrs. Friedgood like a mother to me," she would explain in her broken English. "No. More than a mother. A sister. More than a sister."

Middle-aged, olive-skinned, she was a frail and sickly
woman. When she was sick, Friedgood himself treated her: a
few years before, when she needed an operation because of
gallstones, "the doctor," as she reverentially called him, had
personally put her into a semiprivate room at Lefferts General
Hospital. Coincidentally, she shared the room with Suzie
Bren, on whom Friedgood was also operating.

For the last year Lydia had not been living at 47 Beverly Road but in Corona, Queens, with her children, whom she had finally been able to bring from Santo Domingo. Five mornings a week, she left her home at seven o'clock to arrive at the Friedgoods' by seven-thirty, which allowed her time to clean the kitchen of the remains of Sophie's midnight snacks, then to serve the doctor his grapefruit and orange juice when he came down for breakfast at eight o'clock. Usually there would be a note from Mrs. Friedgood telling Lydia what time to awaken her. Mrs. Friedgood had not been well lately. She suffered from headaches and pains in her back. Usually she slept until noon.

Lydia had not been well, either. She suffered from an allergy—hay fever (or "high fever," as she pronounced it). Friedgood prescribed antihistamine pills for her. After she served the doctor his breakfast, she took one of her pills. But the pills made her drowsy. After the doctor left for the hospital, she would go into the living room, which was below the master bedroom, and lie down on the couch. That way, if Mrs. Friedgood awoke before noon, Lydia could hear her walking about. Though she might have considered herself one of the family, Lydia was afraid of being caught sleeping on the couch when she should have been working.

At seven-thirty Wednesday, as she always did, Lydia let herself into the house through the back door. She washed a few dishes left in the sink from the day before, then wrapped some leftover roast beef and corn. She got Dr. Friedgood's grapefruit ready, but he did not appear; not until nine o'clock, an hour later than usual, did he come down the stairs.

"Don't wake Mrs. Friedgood," he told her. "She has a headache. I gave her something for it." He sat down, and she served him his grapefruit. "How are you feeling today?" the doctor asked her.

"Not so good, Doctor," she answered. Her pills had run out. Only one remained.

While the doctor ate his breakfast Lydia walked upstairs to Beth's old room and took her last pill. Then she lay down on the bed. Moments later she heard the doctor's footsteps on the stairs. She sat up. He handed her a new prescription and walked back down the stairs.

From the window she watched him walk out the door, get into his Cadillac, and back it out of the driveway. Then, after his car pulled away, she walked outside to her own car, took out some laundry from the back seat, and carried it to the basement.

Listening to the washing machine churning, she thought she heard the telephone ringing. She was not certain, however: in the basement the telephone rang only faintly, like a soft *brrr,* in a little box on the wall. She was not feeling well again today. Her allergy was bothering her. The medication was making her drowsy. When the wash was completed, she walked back upstairs to the living room, lay down on the couch, and fell asleep.

She thought she slept only a few minutes. She thought she heard a radio playing and Mrs. Friedgood walking around upstairs. She looked at her watch: ten-thirty. She decided to go up to see whether Mrs. Friedgood was awake.

She walked up the back stairs, past the cartons piled up in the hall, past the piles of books and boxes lying on the floor, into the bathroom next to the master bedroom. The first thing Mrs. Friedgood did when she awoke was take a shower. Lydia always knew when Mrs. Friedgood was up because she left the wet towel she had dried herself with on the bathroom floor for Lydia to pick up.

But the bathroom was empty. There was no Mrs. Friedgood. No towel on the floor. Lydia was surprised.

She walked into the dressing room off the bedroom. But nobody was there, either. The door to the master bedroom was ajar and she peeked inside. Mrs. Friedgood was still in bed, asleep on her side, it seemed. She was facing away from

Lydia, her body covered with a sheet. The sheet was pulled up to her neck and her feet were sticking out.

Lydia shook her head again, surprised. Mrs. Friedgood was still asleep. She turned, walked back downstairs to the living room, lay down on the couch, and dozed off again.

/ ii

The telephone was ringing. Lydia pulled herself from the couch to answer it.

"Hi, Lydia," said the voice on the other end of the wire. "Mrs. Goodman. Is Mrs. Friedgood at home?"

Renee Goodman was annoyed. After Sophie had called from the accountant's in Brooklyn last night, she and her husband had waited until after midnight for her and Charles.

"She's sleeping," Lydia answered.

"It's late, Lydia. Wake her up!"

"No, the doctor say she have a headache."

"For crying out loud, Lydia! It's one o'clock! Go upstairs. I'll hold the phone. Wake her up. It's time she got up!"

Lydia walked up the stairs again to the bedroom. She opened the door and walked inside. The room was hot and stuffy. The shades were pulled down. The windows were closed. The air conditioner was turned off. Mrs. Friedgood was still asleep.

Lydia walked over to the bed and shook her. Her shoulder felt cold and wet. Her feet were still sticking outside the sheet and Lydia began to massage them. She picked up the telephone in the bedroom. "She no hear me," she said to Mrs. Goodman. "Mrs. Friedgood no waking up."

"Lydia, shake her!" Renee Goodman shouted to her.

"I shake her! Mrs. Friedgood no answer."

"Lydia! Shake her! Hit her! Move her!"

Lydia put her hands on Mrs. Friedgood's shoulders and one of her legs. "I try! But she won't move!" For the first time she noticed Mrs. Friedgood's lips and nails. They were blue, almost purplish.

"Mrs. Friedgood, wake up! Wake up, Mrs. Friedgood! Mrs. Goodman calling you!" She picked up the phone. "She won't move! I try but she won't move!"

"Lydia, quick! Hang up the phone. I'm going to call the police. You call Doctor Friedgood."

Renee Goodman hung up and began dialing the police emergency number. She dialed 611. Realizing her mistake, she hung up and dialed again, this time 911. "This is Renee Goodman," she told the police operator. "There's somebody either dead or dying at Forty-seven Beverly Road, Kensington. Get there quickly."

She ran out of her house and jumped into her car. Again she thought of Sophie's phone call to her from the accountant's last night and their not showing up. She and Charles were just leaving, Sophie had said. They would be there around ten-thirty.

That fuck, Renee Goodman thought as she backed her car out of the driveway and started driving north across the Island toward Great Neck. That fuck just killed my friend.

/ iii

Patrolman Bill Glandt of the Kensington Police Department was checking parking-meter violations on North Drive, two blocks away, when the call came over the police radio for a possible DOA at 47 Beverly Road. Bill Glandt was a tall, sandy-haired man, pleasant-looking in a vacuous sort of way. He was in his early forties, and had been a cop in Kensington for twenty years, one of six patrolmen who covered the two-square-mile village and served as a backup for Great Neck Estates, the neighboring village across Middleneck Road, which was on the same police radio band as Kensington.

Not that there was much work to do in either village,

hardly enough—some critics thought—to justify the Kensington policemen's $20,000-plus yearly salary, set at parity with the Nassau County police force, which paid the highest salaries in the country. It was the county force that was responsible for investigating all major crimes in villages like Kensington; the village force dealt mainly with the kinds of complaints that made up the Kensington police blotter for the month of June 1975: two automobile accidents, one of which involved a collision with a parked car; a woman who had slipped and sprained her wrist; a noisy party on Beverly Road; a strange noise at 6 North Drive that was later discovered to come from the exhaust pipe of a vacuum-cleaner system; and twelve burglar alarms, all tripped accidentally by the homeowners themselves.

Still, despite what could be termed at best a humdrum existence, Patrolman Bill Glandt had somehow over the years managed to get himself into serious difficulty, not once but twice. Four years before, he had been severely beaten by two youths as he questioned them about the vandalism of a nearby auto. And six months before, he had, while making the rounds of a vacant house late one night, been shot in the stomach by a burglar.

According to the Kensington police log of Wednesday, June 18, Glandt arrived at 47 Beverly Road at one-thirty-one P.M. He was met at the door by Lydia Fernandez, who was, Glandt reported, "hysterical. She was talking so many languages I could hardly understand what she was saying." Finally it got through to him to go upstairs to the master bedroom.

He followed Lydia up the front stairs, past the boxes and cartons in the hallway. "The house was a mess," Glandt would later remark, as though surprised. "A doctor, you know, is a step above a lot of people," he would explain. Somehow this was not the way he expected a doctor to live.

Entering the bedroom, he was struck by how untidy it was: in one corner Glandt noticed a metal laundry bar with women's clothing hanging from it. And it was hot in the room. The shades drawn. The windows closed. The air conditioner off. Standing in the doorway, he was beginning to perspire. He looked down at the woman lying on the bed. The sheet had been pulled back from her. She lay naked, exposed, a heavy, middle-aged woman. He felt uncomfortable. He tried to avert his eyes. He noticed the sheets. They had, he noticed, a pattern of large yellow flowers with brown stems.

He leaned down over the body. Her hand was underneath her head. Her face lay on the inside of her hand like a baby's. He took hold of the wrist and felt her pulse. None. He touched the body. It was cold. He felt the fingers. They were stiff. He turned to Lydia, who was standing behind him.

"She's dead," he said.

With that, Lydia became more hysterical. She threw herself onto the bed on her hands and knees, and began jumping up and down that way, calling out, "Mrs. Friedgood! Mrs. Friedgood!" Glandt tried to lead her out of the bedroom. Then he noticed the telephone. He decided he had better call a doctor. But it was a warm, sunny Wednesday afternoon and, as Glandt put it, on warm, sunny Wednesday afternoons, "all the doctors in Great Neck are out playing golf."

Instead, because he did not want to touch anything in the room, he walked downstairs and dialed the local volunteer Vigilant Ambulance Service and Fire Company. Founded at the turn of the century by William K. Vanderbilt, who liked to dress up in firefighting gear and drive through the village putting out fires with the locals, the company was staffed by young men, some of whom qualified as ambulance medical technicians, or paramedics, who could as easily defibrillate a heart that had stopped beating as take a pulse.

As he was about to dial he noticed a piece of paper by the phone. It had Dr. Friedgood's phone number, the number of his answering service. He decided to dial it as well.

"The doctor has already been notified," a woman's

voice answered. "Mrs. Friedgood, you know, had a history of strokes."

With that, Glandt returned to the bedroom. This time he lifted the sheet and covered the body of Sophie Friedgood up to the neck. He didn't feel it was proper to leave her uncovered and exposed. He didn't want anyone seeing a doctor's wife naked like that.

At one-forty-two two young men from Hook and Ladder 83 of the Vigilant Ambulance Service and Fire Company arrived at the Friedgood home. Glandt met them at the front door. He led them upstairs to the bedroom. As one of them leaned over the body and felt the carotid artery in the neck, the other took the pulse. The dead woman's hand now, Glandt noticed, was clenched, rigid. She had been dead for some time, he thought.

One of the young men took out a stethoscope, walked around to the far side of the bed, and placed it on Sophie's chest. After a minute he stood up, walked to the phone, and dialed. "Hey, Bob, we can't get any pulse," Glandt heard him say into the phone. With that, the two young men left the bedroom, walked back downstairs and out the door.

Moments later Renee Goodman arrived.

"I'm a friend of the family," she announced to Glandt, then brushed by him to go over to the stairs, where Lydia sat crying.

Just then Glandt saw a white Cadillac pull into the driveway. A tall, lean, curly-haired man with glasses, who Glandt assumed must be Dr. Friedgood, was walking toward the house.

Glandt rushed outside. He didn't know who had notified him but he wanted to be the first person at the house to meet the doctor, to make certain the doctor was properly told the tragic news about his wife.

"Where is she?" Friedgood asked him. Glandt noticed he was carrying a brown zippered case, like a briefcase.

"In bed," Glandt answered.

"In bed? She's still in bed?"

"Oh, Charles," cried Renee, rushing up to him, past Glandt, overcome with loss. "Oh, Charles, I'm sorry, I'm so sorry."

"I've seen death so many times," Friedgood said. "But I never—" His voice broke. He began to run up the stairs.

"Don't let him go up alone," Glandt whispered to Renee. Quickly she followed him, Glandt behind her, Lydia behind him.

They all stood at the edge of the room as Friedgood walked over to the body. He placed his briefcase down on the night table and rolled the body over on its back. He pulled down the sheet and put his ear to the chest. He felt for a pulse. Then he let out a moan. "My Sophie," be began to sob. "My Sophie, my Sophie. She's dead." He bent down, kissed her flush on the lips, then burst into tears.

Glandt tried to lead him away from the bed and out of the room.

Suddenly, as they walked into the hallway, Renee Goodman shouted, "Charles!" They turned and stared at her.

"Charles! Cover her!"

Friedgood walked back into the bedroom and pulled the sheet over Sophie again. When he came out he was carrying two sheets of paper, one white and one yellow.

They all walked downstairs to the living room. "Charles, why didn't you come last night?" Glandt heard Renee ask him in a whisper.

"Sophie wasn't feeling well," Friedgood answered, his voice still quivering. "She had a headache at Lundy's. She had been drinking. We went right home."

Friedgood then picked up the local telephone directory and began searching for the number of a funeral chapel. Glandt noticed on the back cover of the directory the name of the nearby North Shore Chapels.

"Here," he said to Friedgood, pointing to the name.

"My wife has expired," he heard Friedgood say into the telephone. "Can someone come and pick up the body? I have two New York City death certificates with me because I was expecting a patient in Brooklyn to die. Are they good in Nassau?"

There was a pause. "When you come," Glandt heard Friedgood say, "you can bring the proper death-certificate forms and I'll sign them."

"She had a history of strokes," Friedgood said to Glandt as though in explanation. Explanation of what? Glandt wondered. "Her family is in Hazleton, Pennsylvania. That's where she wanted to be buried."

Then, once again, he picked up the telephone. This time he began calling his children to tell them to return home immediately. "According to Jewish law," he said to Glandt, "she has to be buried by sundown tomorrow."

Part IV

THE CASE

17

ON WEDNESDAY, JUNE 18, 1975, RAYMOND SICKLES, chief of the Kensington Police Department, was at a luncheon at the Hotel Statler Hilton in New York City, accepting the Automobile Club of New York's annual Pedestrian Safety Award because Kensington had been forty-three years without a traffic fatality. Raymond Sickles, six feet two inches tall, in his early sixties and just a year from retirement, had lived in the area longer than all of Kensington's doctors, lawyers, and businessmen, in a small, rented house outside the village's boundaries. He had joined the department nearly forty years before, in 1936, at a salary of $142.50 a month, and, residents felt, he seemed to feel a special responsibility for the village and for all of them. In his time he had discovered moonshine stills and had delivered babies. At least one mother was so grateful for his assistance, so the story went, that she named the child he had delivered after him. In his retirement speech, the following year, which was written up in the local paper, he complained he had little regard for modern gadgetry such as radar guns or infrared night-vision surveillance. He believed, he told his audience, in good, old-fashioned police work. And as if to bear this out, though he had been chief for the last twenty-odd years, Sickles still insisted on doing target practice, patrolled the village itself twice a day, and made certain his men did the same.

He had little use for most of his subordinates. "Nobody ever shot *me* in the dark," he liked to say. Once, when a cop was not performing to Sickles' satisfaction, Sickles appeared late at night at the station in neighboring Great Neck Estates, where the fellow had claimed he'd be patrolling. But Sickles found him asleep in his patrol car and brought him up on departmental charges. The village elders eventually dropped the case, but they appreciated Sickles all the more.

With him, wherever he patrolled, he brought his German shepherd, a massive, marvelously well-trained animal that Sickles kept in the back of his station wagon, where the dog slept during the day. One summer the village had been troubled by kids swimming at midnight in the village pool. Whenever the cops chased them, the kids outran them. Finally the village elders decided that something must be done. Sickles was summoned. "I'll stop them," he said.

The next week he was at the pool every night with the dog. Late one night he spotted a gang of teenagers, boys and girls, jumping into the pool nude. Sickles watched them swimming. Then he and the dog walked to the edge of the pool. Sickles picked up their clothes. While the dog growled, Sickles shone his giant flashlight at them and announced they were all under arrest. "The first one who runs," he announced, "the dog gets." One by one, naked, their hands up over their heads, they came out of the pool.

Whenever he appeared in village traffic court his testimony was impeccable. "His car was parked two and a half feet from the curb," he would recite. Or "The car approached at ten miles per hour." He would remember the color of traffic lights, direct quotes of suspects. "I defy anyone to cross-examine him," a village commissioner of public safety remarked years later. "His testimony was always perfect. Whether it was true was something else again."

And Sickles was expert at ingratiating himself with the villagers. When off duty, he did jobs for people. Besides being a cop, he had a hack license and often served as a chauffeur, driving Kensington residents to the airport, to the city, or—if they had business dealings there—into a rough neighborhood to collect a payment. One resident had had trouble with his partners, who were threatening to evict him from his business. He had Sickles drive him to his office, then introduced Sickles to his partners as "my driver and our chief of police." He never, so the story went, had trouble with his partners afterward.

Yet though he was always doing favors, he never had his hand out. Even at Christmas he never asked for tips, though villagers made sure never to forget him. If someone had a problem he was always there. If someone was locked out of the house; if there was a family argument; if a resident thought he saw a prowler; if there was a party and guests overstayed the two-hour parking limit on the street and a cop issued a ticket by mistake—all it would take to straighten it out was a call to Sickles.

In fact Sickles had had difficulty with only one man, a retired business executive who became Kensington's mayor. So irritated did Sickles become at him that he abruptly quit the force and for the next three years drove a cab around the area. But his successor, chosen from the ranks, did not run the tight ship Sickles had. Unlike Sickles, he did not live in the area. Each day, when his tour was over, he simply left for home.

Soon there were grumblings about the police, who were not performing as well as they had under Sickles. Sickles had seemed to be there anytime there was a burglary. Residents had trusted him with their keys. Now burglaries seemed to be increasing. When the mayor died three years later, Sickles was asked to return as chief.

He did, at his previous salary of twelve thousand dollars a year. Then the superintendent of maintenance developed cancer. Sickles told the village board to keep him on the payroll, that he would do that man's job as well as his own. For the next year he supervised the street cleaners as well as his cops. At the end of the year the village voted him a thousand-dollar raise.

/ ii

It was late Wednesday afternoon when Sickles returned from New York City with the Auto Club of New York's Pedestrian Safety Award. He went directly to the Kensington police booth at the edge of the village that served as headquarters.

"Anything happen?" he asked Patrolman Bill Glandt, who was just coming off duty.

"Sophie Friedgood died," Glandt answered.

"Oh? Nice lady," Sickles said vaguely. He did not know the Friedgoods well, although he had heard gossip about them, of course. About the only thing he remembered about them was an incident that had occurred years before. They had been summoned to village court because neighbors complained that a dog they owned was always left in the backyard and never stopped barking. In court Mrs. Friedgood and the children had gotten into a shouting match with the neighbors. But when Friedgood arrived (he was an hour late) he had been all smiles and innocence. "Why didn't you call me?" he had said to everyone. "I'd have taken care of everything."

"What happened to her?" Sickles now said to Glandt.

"Stroke," Glandt answered.

"Did they take her to the hospital?" Sickles asked.

"No," said Glandt.

"Who was the doctor who signed the death certificate?"

"Dr. Friedgood."

"What?" asked Sickles sharply. "Dr. Friedgood?" There is an unwritten rule—not a law, but a custom—that those who deal with death, like doctors and policemen, all adhere to: no matter what the circumstances, a cop does not permit a doctor to sign the death certificate for someone in his own family.

Sickles stood up from his chair. "How could you let that happen?" he shouted at Glandt.

/ iii

That night there was a monthly village board meeting Sickles had to attend. The meeting began at eight. Sickles read the May police report and displayed the plaque given him by the Automobile Club. There was a discussion as to the advisability of purchasing a radar gun for the police department to catch speeding vehicles; the public-works report for May was read; a resident gave a report of why and how he did crack-sealing work at the Kensington park and pool. The mayor promised that formal recognition of his services would be made at the next board meeting.

Sickles, however, was not listening. He found himself thinking about Sophie Friedgood.

The village justice reports for the months of April and May were read. The mayor announced the progress of a suit against the village, over property assessments. The mayor read a letter from the North Shore Community Art Center, which asked for permanent funding from individual villages for the center as a community organization.

Sickles looked at his watch. He could not get Sophie Friedgood out of his mind. It wasn't just the business with the death certificate—there was something else.

The mayor promised to get in touch with the chief of the Nassau traffic department to change the traffic signals in Great Neck Plaza so that traffic was rerouted away from Kensington. A letter was read requesting a 50-percent rebate of the annual village property tax for elderly residents who had lived in Kensington a long time, regardless of their income.

Sickles looked at his watch again. It was nearly eleven-thirty. Something about the death of Sophie Friedgood rankled. Something about it made him uneasy. He couldn't think why—the poor woman's body had been taken away, and the next day she would be both dead *and* buried.

There was a discussion about painting traffic signals at Arleigh and Beverly roads; about painting crosswalk signs at the school intersections; about changing the light at the Kensington gate and Middlesex Road to speed up the number of cars exiting from the village.

The discussion ended. The mayor stood up. The meeting was over. At last. Sickles sighed and looked at his watch. It was eleven-forty-five.

Alone, he walked back to the police booth and began reading the blotter again. There was something about Sophie Friedgood's death. Something he couldn't quite grasp.

Then it came to him. Sitting in the police booth, alone, after midnight, he remembered the call a few months before from Friedgood's daughter. She had called because her father and mother were fighting. He had driven over to their house on Beverly Road, but it had been nothing. Now, again late at night, he remembered the words the daughter had used when she called. Her mother, she had said, said her husband was going to kill her.

/ iv

At eight A.M. the next morning Sickles knocked at the office door of Dr. William Kaplan, on Nassau Drive. Like Sickles, Kaplan was an old-timer in Kensington. He was a general practitioner, in his seventies and still practicing, and in fact was in the process of taking blood from a patient when he heard the knock. Since he was not expecting any more patients that morning, Kaplan was surprised. "Who's there?" he called out.

"Chief Sickles."

"I'll be right there, Chief."

"Doctor, I want to talk to you."

Kaplan stepped into his outer office. He was surprised when Sickles closed the door behind him. "I want your advice," Sickles began. "Mrs. Friedgood died yesterday. I was off. You know a little about Friedgood. I would appreciate your opinion. He pronounced her dead and he signed the death certificate. I wonder—"

Later, Kaplan would claim he had never met Friedgood, that he had only heard rumors about him. "Do you think I should notify the Nassau County police?" Sickles asked him.

"You get right on the phone," Kaplan answered.

18

THE NASSAU COUNTY POLICE DEPARTMENT HEAD-
quarters is a long, rectangular, boxlike building, shapeless and
graceless, which sprawls from the old courthouse in Mineola,
the county seat, south to the giant parking lots of Saks and
Bloomingdale's in adjacent Garden City. The police force that
occupies it was started in 1925, when the county consisted
only of potato farms, the South Shore fishing villages, and the
Gold Coast, the North Shore estates. Its first commissioner had
been a retired New York City police lieutenant, hand-picked
by the Nassau County Republican leader, and his fifty-five-
man force consisted of some foot patrolmen, a motorcycle
contingent, and a former photographer from the New York
Daily News who was reported to be a fingerprint expert and
who supposedly provided the department with "technologi-
cal" advice.

Fifty years later Nassau County's population numbered
1.5 million and the department had become the second-larg-
est police force in the state, the seventh largest in the nation.
On paper, at least, its standards were the highest. Its salaries
were the highest in the country. And except for such ageless

police rights as that of walking into the kitchen of a restaurant and glomming a free meal, or playing eighteen holes of free golf at country clubs on the one day each week the clubs were closed to their members, the department prided itself on being corruption-free.

Still, as the fiefdom of the Nassau Republican Party, which appointed as police chief one political crony after another, it would always be unfavorably compared to the New York City Police Department. On its fiftieth anniversary, newspaper accounts would still refer to an incident that had occurred in the basement of the old headquarters building during Prohibition. A dozen officers—including Oyster Bay's then most prominent Republican, who had been appointed a deputy police chief just six months before—were charged with stomping to death a small-time bootlegger named Hymie Stark. Stark had made the mistake of mugging an old woman whose son happened to be a Nassau County detective. The police officers all refused to testify against one another at the grand-jury hearing, and the grand jury failed to indict. The Oyster Bay Republican gracefully retired as deputy chief, and the cops—who had been suspended after the stamping incident—were all reinstated, heroes to the department and to the local citizenry.

The Detective Division had a slightly more glamorous record. It had achieved something of a nationwide reputation during the postwar years by presumably solving two celebrated murders. The first was the slaying of Gold Coast millionaire sportsman William Woodward, who was shot on his Oyster Bay Cove estate at two-nine on Sunday morning, October 30, 1955, by his wife, Ann, who claimed she had mistaken him for a prowler. The two, it was said at the time, were near divorce.

The Woodwards were part of the North Shore horsey set—he was the owner and breeder of a number of top-class racehorses, among them the Belmont Stakes winner Nashua. Their friends included the Duke and Duchess of Windsor, both of whom were interviewed by Nassau detectives. Under pressure for a quick arrest, detectives arrested a twenty-three-year-old German immigrant named Paul Wirths, who had recently been convicted of a string of North Shore burglaries. After two days of questioning by a young detective sergeant named Ed Curran, Wirths admitted to having attempted to burglarize the Woodward home the night Ann Woodward shot her husband.

William Woodward's death was ruled accidental. Wirths was tried and convicted of trespassing, then swiftly deported. For years rumors persisted that Ann Woodward had paid off both Wirths and the police.

A year later the department acted less swiftly in an equally sensational case, the kidnapping of Peter Weinberger, an infant who had been snatched from the front porch of his house in Westbury; a peculiarly printed note demanding a ransom of two thousand dollars had been left in his carriage. The kidnapping law at that time did not require local police departments to request FBI assistance until a week had passed. Nassau police did not invite the FBI into the case until then.

For the next two months hundreds of FBI agents under the New York City bureau chief, James J. Kelly, worked together with hundreds of Nassau detectives under the same detective sergeant, Ed Curran, who had obtained Wirths' confession in the Woodward case. After examining thousands of handwriting samples, comparing driver's-license signatures to the peculiar writing on the ransom note, authorities finally came upon the name of Angelo LaMarca, an unemployed mechanic on the South Shore. LaMarca led police to the baby's shallow grave along the Northern State Parkway. He had been abandoned just a few hundred yards from the Weinberger home.

The department's troubles weren't over when LaMarca was booked. Kelly insisted he be brought to New York City, where the FBI would have jurisdiction when it came time for trial. But Nassau authorities wanted LaMarca tried locally. A team of Nassau detectives was sent to FBI headquarters in New York with orders not to return without him. LaMarca was tried and convicted in Nassau and electrocuted in Sing Sing.

Five years later, after Nassau's then police commissioner parked his car on a South Shore bridge near Jones Beach and jumped into the swift tidal waters, James J. Kelly retired from the FBI and was appointed Nassau County police commissioner. When the chief of detectives resigned, Kelly appointed as his successor young Detective Sergeant Ed Curran, whom he promoted over the heads of dozens of other senior ranking officers.

Fourteen years later, long after Kelly had retired, and long after his successor and *his* successor had retired as well, Curran still remained as chief of detectives. In fact he was in his office on the Thursday morning of June 19, 1975, when a call came into police headquarters in Mineola reporting on the death of Sophie Friedgood. Curran did not take the call. There was no murder, no cause for the chief of detectives to become involved. There was only a suspicious death that might need looking into. Instead the call—like any report of an unexplained death—went directly to Homicide.

/ ii

Detective Thomas Palladino was not supposed to be working that Thursday. Like many other Nassau County police officers, he had a second job. Over the years he had sold real estate, dealt in used cars, and driven a hearse. He had been scheduled to drive the hearse that Thursday morning. But Bill Conigsby, who was supposed to have been "squealing," or catching cases, in Homicide, had called in sick. At the last minute Tommy Palladino had been prevailed upon to come to police headquarters to squeal in his place.

He was Mr. Nice Guy, Palladino. At least that was the

impression he liked to leave with people. Not just the detectives with whom he worked but the public with whom he dealt—the friends or families of victims who died in car crashes or under the tracks of the Long Island Rail Road, who died naturally, or accidentally, or otherwise. No matter whom he interviewed—suspects included—he seemed to be smiling, almost laughing. The most incriminating statements he solicited from murderers or their accomplices he appeared to accept so casually as to shrug off, almost to turn into a joke.

He was a burly man with wavy blond hair that was thinning in back and that he combed and patted down more carefully than he would have done a few years before. He was in his late thirties, though he liked to give his age as a few years younger. He liked to think he was different from the other guys in Homicide, who, to a man, considered themselves the *crème de la crème* of the Detective Division—or, as they, to a man, pronounced it, "the cream de la cream."

And at least on the surface he was different. Certainly he was different from the stolid, gray-haired Andreoli, the dean of the squad, a grandfather now in his sixties; or the flashy Cardone, who had once told an interviewer he wanted to be a detective in Homicide because of "the glamour"; or the legendary Bonora, who was forced to leave the squad after accusing Nassau's flamboyant district attorney, Bill Cahn, of lying about evidence in a murder case; or Guido, who was so brilliant he completed law school while squad commander, finishing second in his class, then was police commissioner for two years until the Republicans dismissed him because he refused to play ball with the PBA, with whom the politicians had made a deal for the next election.

No, Palladino was different from all of them. People, that was his game. He cared about people. He genuinely liked people, he would say. He wanted them to like him. Usually they did. Often they ended up spilling their guts to him.

He had grown up in Brooklyn, and his first full-time job

had been driving a hearse used by a Jewish funeral home, a job that had filled his speech with all sorts of Yiddish expressions, which he would use as inventively as he did most of his English. Often he would drive out to the cemetery with the family of the deceased, the body in the rear of the hearse, the bereaved seated beside him in the front of the hearse in tears. Usually by the time they reached the cemetery Palladino was in tears as well.

"I'm all bullshitter," he liked to say of himself. "I talk apples, pears, oranges for half an hour before I get around to the subject." His fellow detectives had another name for him. They called him "the Golden Tongue."

His greatest asset, he liked to think, was his empathy. He was simpatico. It was not a word *he* would have used; he preferred "relating," relating to anybody—rich, poor, young, old; doctors or orderlies; welfare recipients or rich suburban housewives.

At the beginning of the Friedgood case when he interviewed Renee Goodman, he noticed how nervous, how afraid she seemed of him. Standing in the doorway of her custom-built ranch house in a development in the Five Towns area, where prices for houses began at $100,000, he saw a tall, darkly attractive, well-groomed woman, and he sensed instinctively he was probably the first police officer she had ever spoken to. Trying to put her at ease, smiling as he patted his hair in the back, the first thing he said to her was, "If they make a movie, who would you want to play your part?"

"Anne Bancroft," Renee answered.

He had joined the Nassau County Police Department in 1960, at age twenty-three, when the salary for a rookie was $4,700 a year. Yet Palladino had always managed. With his second job—he was selling used cars then and would later purchase a couple of "mother-and-daughter" houses for resale—he bought himself a secondhand Cadillac, or "Jew canoe," as some described it around headquarters. His wife—by police standards he had married late, in his late twenties—owned her own beauty salon. That year they had purchased a split-level home in Huntington on a half-acre plot with a pond. He had two children whom he guarded zealously, as did all homicide detectives, who had seen so many accidental deaths involving small children. For Tommy Palladino, life had not been bad. Not bad at all.

/ iii

Shortly before noon on the day after Sophie Friedgood's body was discovered, Palladino was called into the office of the squad commander, Captain William Meddis. Meddis—tall, ramrod-straight, with a crew cut, the professional-looking cop—could not have been more unlike his subordinate. The squad commander was known for his meticulous note-taking: "Suspect arrived at what time; got out of which door of his car; stayed on premises for how long; was accompanied by...." Never an unnecessary word. Never a personal word. With Meddis nothing was personal. Everything was strictly business.

That is why Tommy Palladino merely looked at Meddis and said nothing when that Thursday morning Meddis—who had been on the telephone for the past hour—suddenly said to him, "You better call home. You're going on a trip. Go to the main office and get a map of Pennsylvania. We've got to pick up someone from the DA's office. I'll explain it to you on the way. And when you get the map, look up the town of Hazleton."

19

WHEN IT WAS ALL OVER, WHAT DEBBIE WOULD remember from that first night after her mother's death was an indefinable feeling. She and Avi had driven half the night from Gloucester, Massachusetts, where they were working that summer, and arrived in Kensington at one A.M. that Thursday morning. Driving past the darkened houses on Beverly Road, pulling into the driveway of her home, and walking through the front door, certainly "suspicion" had seemed to her like too strong a word. Probably what she sensed was uneasiness. Or perhaps it was simply her imagination at work, stimulated by the superstitions of the old Jewish writer who had come to be part of her—his demons, *golems*, portents, and signs. But afterward, when she was tormented by the dreams that would cause her to wake screaming in the night, she would remember every detail of that first night home in Kensington. It was as if she were in a silent movie on slow-motion film, the camera following her from room to room, dwelling here, pausing there, recording her and her father's every movement. Later she would say that from the first she had sensed something was very, very wrong.

Opening the front door, she had been at first overcome by emotion. The first person she saw was Esther, in bed in her old room. They hugged and kissed and began to cry.

Then her father walked into the bedroom. She felt him tap her on the shoulder and she turned and they embraced. Together they all walked into Beth's room, where earlier in the day Lydia had sat on the bed after taking the antihistamine pill that had made her drowsy. They woke up Beth and all of them began to cry.

"Can a stroke come suddenly, Papa?" Debbie asked her father.

"With a stroke, a hemorrhage is not uncommon," he began to explain. "It can only be stopped if you catch it before it hits the brain. If I could have caught it in time, it wouldn't have killed her.

"She was having severe headaches the night before," he continued. "She had been drinking lots of wine at Lundy's. I gave her two Empirin before she went to bed. Then she went to sleep, and that's when the stroke must have come on."

Presently her father and Esther returned to their rooms. Debbie remained to talk with Beth. She lost track of the time, but later still, she and Beth decided to go together to their parents' room to sit on their parents' double bed. If they sat on the bed, Debbie remembered thinking, it would seem as though her mother were still alive.

The door to her parents' bedroom was closed, but they did not knock. Opening it, they saw their father. He was sitting on the bed, their mother's pocketbooks strewn about, and he was going through them, picking out papers, stuffing those he wanted into one of the pocketbooks. As Beth and Debbie came into the room he looked up, startled. "I've got to start cleaning up around here," he mumbled, as if to himself. "I've got to start cleaning up."

He sat down in a chair while Debbie and Beth sat together on the bed and they began to talk about their mother. Forgotten were the fights Beth and Debbie had had with her.

Debbie remembered how healthy and happy she had seemed recently; how her mother had changed so much toward her in the last year, as though she were coming to know her for the first time. Forgotten, too, were the ugly arguments her parents had had. Instead Debbie said to her father, "What a shock her death must have been to you. What a terrible thing after all these years it must be for you for her to be gone.

"Was your relationship with Mommy getting better at the end?" she wanted to know. "Was it getting straightened out? Was it starting to get smoother?"

"Oh, well," her father answered, "you know, you always had to try and please her. I was trying not to get her upset. Not to say anything that might upset her."

"Is it going to be hard to sleep in the bed tonight without her?" she asked him.

"Oh, sure," he answered. "Sure it will be. Of course."

"She was so happy and healthy, so full of life. It was such a shock."

"Yes, of course. It is a shock. It is a big shock."

Still later, after she and Beth had returned to their rooms, Debbie could not sleep. In the middle of the night she decided to return once more to her parents' room. Afterward she would remember how she had silently opened the bedroom door, still half expecting to see her mother sleeping in the bed, still not fully believing her mother was dead.

Instead she saw her father. He was asleep in the middle of their double bed. He was lying on his back, his eyes closed, his mouth open, snoring contentedly. Later she would say, "It was then that something clicked."

/ ii

The next morning she confided her uneasiness to Avi, and he echoed her feelings. Earlier, while Debbie and the others were asleep, he and Jack Cook, Beth's husband, the doctor, had driven together to Kennedy Airport to pick up Stephen, who was flying home from Santo Domingo, where he was attending medical school. As they drove, Avi had turned to Jack. "Sophie was healthy," he said to him. "You are a doctor. Do you think there is something strange about her death?"

Jack, he remembered, had turned and looked at him as he drove, and said nothing. Avi felt he agreed.

So he and Debbie decided to watch, to listen to every word her father said. That same morning, Toba took Debbie aside and told her she had gone into their parents' room and found their father writing a letter on an aerogram. Seeing her, he had stood up, pushing the letter aside, trying to cover it with his arm.

"Is that a letter to our cousins in Israel?" Toba asked.

"Yes. Yes, it is," he answered. "My uncle is a rabbi there, you know." With that he had taken a book from the shelves and covered the letter. Debbie began to wonder.

Stephen was exhausted from his night flight home, and tried to catch a little sleep on the living-room couch after he, Avi, and Jack arrived home. But at nine o'clock that morning, his father awakened him and drove him to the banks to close out some of Sophie's separate bank accounts. And Debbie wondered.

When she came down to breakfast, she heard Beth's and Jack's voices. "You shouldn't have done that, Papa," Beth was saying. "You shouldn't have signed the death certificate."

"It is not a law," her father answered. "Doctors don't do it but it is not a law."

"But doctors don't *do* it," said Jack.

"There is no law against it," her father repeated.

Later that morning, just before they were to leave for Hazleton, Debbie decided to speak to Esther, the lawyer. She was in the bathroom putting on her makeup and brushing her long blond hair. Debbie began telling her about the night before, about coming into their parents' bedroom and finding their father going through their mother's pocketbook; of returning later to the bedroom by herself and seeing their father asleep on his back, snoring contentedly. She told her how their father had taken Stephen with him to the banks that morning to close out their mother's accounts; of what Jack had said at breakfast about the death certificate.

"I'm afraid," said Debbie. "Mommy was so healthy. . . ."

Suddenly Esther turned and glared at Debbie. "Suspicion! Suspicion! You have suspicions," she began to shout, "but you have no proof! You have no proof!"

On the drive to Hazleton they began to ask their father about an autopsy. They had gone in two cars, in one of them Debbie and Beth, Jack and Avi, Friedgood driving, his mother, Chafke—whom Sophie had forbidden in her house—seated silently beside him. "Papa," Debbie said to him, "was there any sign the night before? Wasn't there any indication? Wasn't there anything anyone could do?"

"Nothing," he answered.

"But it was so sudden. Couldn't we find out how she died? Couldn't we have an autopsy?"

"No," he answered. "There's no need for it. I'm sure of the cause. She had a history of strokes. There is nothing we could learn from an autopsy that I haven't told you. If there was any need to do it I would have, but there is no need."

"But, Papa," said Beth, "I really don't want to have Mommy buried without knowing for sure how she died. How long would an autopsy take?"

"About a half hour to an hour."

"That's enough time. And I think it is important."

But as they pulled up at the home of their relatives on Aspen Street, the conversation ceased. Her father turned off the motor and they all got out. Nothing more was said about an autopsy.

20

IT WAS A FOUR-HOUR DRIVE TO HAZLETON. ACROSS the Throgs Neck Bridge, west over the George Washington Bridge to the new Route 80, across New Jersey, past the Delaware Water Gap, and into the Poconos. They were in Meddis' green Plymouth, Palladino driving, Meddis next to him. Sitting in the back in his somber three-piece suit was Steve Scaring, the young, cocky chief of the DA's Homicide Bureau, who had been chief not quite a year.

It was only as they were driving that Palladino learned what the trip was all about. They were going to a funeral home to try to stop a burial. From his days as a hearse driver, Palladino knew that religious law requires Orthodox Jews to bury their dead quickly, whereas Italians, by custom, wait three days.

Meddis had already notified the Nassau County medical examiner, Dr. Leslie Lukash. Lukash had said the body should be returned to Nassau for a routine autopsy. But there was little chance of that, they knew. If they were lucky they might be able to have an autopsy performed in Hazleton before the funeral. There was nothing to this case, they all agreed as they drove. Most likely, a doctor carelessly signed the death certificate for his wife, then shipped the body out of state for burial. Unusual, perhaps. But not unlawful.

This is ridiculous, Palladino thought as they drove. "What is this?" he said out loud. "Another Sam Sheppard?" They all began to laugh.

/ ii

More than 150 years after it was founded, nearly fifty years after Hyman Davidowitz settled there, the city of Hazleton has become a grimy, gray place, its population dwindling, its industry dying. Its main avenue, Broad Street, passes old red-brick and already abandoned buildings. And the legacy of its once-rich anthracite vein—which follows Route 81 two hundred miles south from Scranton through Hazleton—is the ring of bare, scarred, strip-mined hills surrounding the town.

Fierro's Funeral Home sits in the old section of Hazleton, south of Broad Street. It is a brick building with white columns, built at the turn of the century by the grandparents of the current owner; a newspaper article in the local paper at the time described it as "comparable to any private residence for dignity and refinement."

In the seventy-five years since then, the Fierros have kept the outside the same, but they have added three chapels, two parlors, and a washing room—the latter directly inside the garage door so that a hearse can back in and discharge its contents onto what appears to be a loading ramp.

It was this washing room that had led Hazleton's Jews to Fierro's. Until then, as there was no Jewish undertaker in Hazleton, Orthodox Jews—who are required by religious law to wash a body before it is buried—had washed the bodies at home. Old man Fierro's brother owned a furniture store between Pine and Wyoming in the old Jewish district. When the washing room was built, the Jews began bringing their dead to Fierro's.

It was late in the afternoon when Palladino and Meddis arrived at Fierro's. They had dropped Scaring off at the Hazleton police station to contact the Luzerne County district attorney, to ask him to try to get a court order to stop the burial. Scaring knew he had little chance; they had no evidence of anything improper. "Just tell the doctor I've gone to get a court order," Scaring told Palladino. It was a bluff, but not a lie. "Maybe the doctor will go for it," Scaring said.

About twenty mourners were at the funeral home when Palladino and Meddis arrived. They were milling about the chapels and in Fierro's office, which was off the center hall, waiting for the services to begin.

The rabbi was there as well. As he entered, Palladino felt embarrassed. No law had been broken. At most, it seemed, there had been carelessness. A funeral was about to begin, and they were intruders.

Meddis approached the rabbi. "We're representing Nassau County, New York, at an inquiry by the medical examiner's office," he said stiffly in his official police voice.

The rabbi stared at him questioningly. "The fact that the deceased left the state without a release from the medical examiner's office, without an autopsy being performed . . ."

As he spoke an older man in a dark suit, his curly gray hair partially covered by a *yarmulke,* approached them. Palladino noticed that the man's shoes were unshined. With him was a small, delicate old woman with white hair and milk-white skin.

"I'm Dr. Friedgood," he began. "What's going on here?" Meddis told him. "This is ridiculous," Friedgood protested. "I don't understand what you're doing here. I've been treating my wife for years."

"Perhaps, Dr. Friedgood," replied Meddis, "it was only poor judgment when you signed the death certificate."

"But I've got my family here," said Friedgood. "We can't stop the burial."

"We could," said Meddis slowly, "get a court order to send the body back to Nassau for an autopsy."

"Who's the medical examiner there?" Friedgood demanded.

"Dr. Leslie Lukash."

"Oh, Lukash," Friedgood said, nodding. "I know him. I think he was one of my students. Let me talk to him."

Meddis and Friedgood walked into Fierro's office. Left outside, Palladino was relieved. Let Lukash talk to him, he thought. Standing outside, he could hear only snatches of the conversation. He could see the doctor gesturing. He was struck by how calm he seemed, how steady his hands were.

He saw Meddis hand him the telephone.

"I know you," he heard Friedgood saying to Lukash. "You were one of my students in Brooklyn."

There was a pause. Lukash was obviously saying something to him. "Couldn't we do it here?" he finally heard Friedgood say. He saw Meddis get back on the phone. There were facilities for performing an autopsy at Saint Joseph's Hospital, just three blocks away, Fierro was saying. It meant contacting the local coroner at the Veterans Administration Hospital in Wilkes-Barre.

By then Scaring had arrived. His bluff had worked.

While they waited for the coroner, Scaring had Palladino take a statement from Friedgood. It was routine, Palladino explained. A mere formality.

"By all means," Friedgood said. He was so calm, Palladino noted. No sign of excitement at all.

Friedgood pointed to one of the empty chapels, where they could be alone and not disturb the other mourners. In the corner was the casket of Sophie Friedgood. "Are you sure this is all right here?" Palladino asked him.

"By all means," Friedgood repeated.

The door to the chapel was open. They could see into the foyer. Relatives were still milling about. "Doctor," Palladino began, as tactfully as he could, "I would like to get some information concerning the activities of your wife, some background and circumstances surrounding the death of your wife. . . ."

"I got his pedigree, his name, date of birth, what he did for a living, office telephone numbers," Palladino recalled later. As they spoke, people kept entering, asking Friedgood about the delay.

Friedgood answered all of them calmly, cooperatively. No sign of excitement. No panic. This was simply a slip-up, an unfortunate formality, Friedgood told them. Palladino felt uncomfortable; Friedgood was still calm. Obviously the doctor was telling the truth, Palladino thought. If they could just get it over with and get out of there.

Palladino's glance drifted toward the casket. "Doctor," he began, feeling more than ever like an intruder, "could you start with your activities the day of—"

In all, the statement took up three pages. "My wife complained of a headache," Friedgood explained. "She took some Empirin Compound and went to bed around midnight. A stroke had left her with a weak left side. She was a moderate drinker. We slept in the same bed. We fell asleep immediately. . . . The next morning I kissed my wife good-bye. In her sleepy state she told me she still had a headache. It was the last time I saw her alive. . . .

"By the way," he added when his statement was completed. "I want it known this was my wife's idea to be buried here."

"If you like," Palladino answered, "I'll make a note of that."

By then the coroner had been located. They were to meet him at Saint Joseph's Hospital. Palladino looked at his watch. It was already six-fifteen.

/ iii

The Luzerne County coroner, George Hudock, a short, wiry man dressed in mod slacks and a sports shirt, seemed to Palladino very certain of himself. When Friedgood spotted him he requested a private consultation, alone in the doctors' lounge. Uh-oh, Palladino thought. It always gave him a funny feeling when two doctors went off by themselves.

Fifteen minutes later they reappeared, and Hudock announced he would conduct an autopsy, with his assistant, on the remains of Sophie Friedgood.

"We would like a detective present," Steve Scaring said.

Friedgood turned to Hudock. "They're trying to railroad me," he said.

Uh-oh, thought Palladino again. It was the first sign something might be wrong.

"It's his prerogative," said Hudock. "It's his wife. There will be nobody present except Dr. Friedgood. This is a private autopsy, not a medical examiner's investigation, and Dr. Friedgood is paying for it."

"In New York it is customary for a detective—" Scaring began.

"This is my autopsy," said Hudock.

"We can get a court order," said Scaring.

"By the time you get it I'll have conducted the autopsy," snapped the coroner. With that, Hudock and Friedgood walked inside to the morgue. Hudock locked the door behind them.

Palladino stared after them, perplexed. Both as a detective and as a driver for funeral homes, Palladino had seen literally hundreds of deaths. He had seen children beaten to death by parents. He had seen people after a drug overdose. He had seen people with limbs cut off, drunks mangled under the wheels of the Long Island Rail Road. And he had talked to the survivors afterward. Often they, too, were reluctant to have an autopsy performed. But there was something puzzling here. Usually, he thought, the bereaved's first reaction would be to say to a detective, "It's my wife. I don't want anybody seeing her like that." But Friedgood did not say that. "At no point did he say," as Palladino put it, "that he was averse to a stranger viewing his wife."

And there was something else, something more disturbing. Friedgood may have been a doctor, but Palladino could not remember anyone ever volunteering to watch his own wife being cut up.

/ iv

They were inside for an hour. It was extremely quiet. Scaring stood with his ear to the door. The only noise was of the saw cutting.

Occasionally Hudock's assistant stepped out for a moment, then returned without a word. But each time he came out he caught Palladino's eye.

Then Hudock reappeared. Friedgood walked behind him. Palladino thought he detected a change in Hudock's manner. "I find no detectable cause of death," he announced. "There was no cerebrovascular accident, although there had been one years before. There was no problem with the heart. At this time I would have to call the death suspicious."

"Come on, Doctor," said Scaring, leading Hudock off to the side and away from Friedgood. "What did you find?"

"I told you."

Was it suicide? Palladino asked himself. Was Friedgood trying to hide a drug overdose? He looked over at Friedgood. He was standing by himself, expressionless.

"Come on, Doctor, you must have found something," Scaring persisted. "What about the stomach? Had she eaten recently?"

"I found a full stomach."

"A full stomach?" With their background in homicide,

they all knew that food is digested and the stomach emptied within six hours after a meal. Scaring looked at Palladino. In the statement Palladino had just taken down, Friedgood said he had kissed his wife that morning.

"Maybe she had a midnight snack," Scaring volunteered.

"No," said Hudock. "It was a main meal." Again Scaring looked at Palladino. Since her last meal had been dinner, and since her stomach would have been empty within six hours if she had lived that long, then Sophie Friedgood could not have been alive that morning as Friedgood had said.

"Can we see her?" said Scaring suddenly.

"See the body? You want to look at the body?" But now he did not stop them.

They walked into the morgue. It was a small, hot, muggy room. There was no air conditioning, no fans. The room stank. There were two tables in it, and on one of them the body of Sophie Friedgood lay on its stomach. There were bruises on the buttocks, marks that had now turned dark red. One of them was a perfect circle, the size of a dime.

"Those bruises . . ." said Scaring.

"I mentioned them to the doctor," said Hudock. "The doctor said they were postmortem, from moving the body."

"The doctor said they were postmortem? They came from moving the body? What do you think, Doctor?"

"Clearly," said Hudock, "they are not postmortem."

"Could they be injection sites?" Scaring asked as he and Palladino stared at the body.

"They could be."

"Did you use a magnifying glass to look at them, Doctor?"

"No . . ."

"Did you photograph them, Doctor?"

"No. I . . ."

They turned the body over. There were more markings, more bruises, which appeared to be symmetrical, beneath both arms, on the right thigh, and on her chest. "Doctor, did you see these?"

"I . . ."

"Did you photograph these bruises?"

"No."

"Will you?"

"Yes."

With that, he and Scaring left the room to put in a call to the Pennsylvania state police for a photographer.

Left alone with the assistant, Palladino again glanced down at the body. It was the first time he had really seen Sophie Friedgood. Staring at her, he saw a short, squat woman, a motherly type, he remembered thinking, a homebody, not one of those rich North Shore Jews who was forty-five but dressed like twenty-one, who went shopping at Waldbaum's in her tennis outfit. She was not well made up or well cared for. Her hair was not dyed platinum or frosted. Her fingernails seemed worn and bitten. Money had not been spent on her, he decided. She had let herself go.

He continued to look at her closely. Now he saw black-and-blue marks under her arms. Hudock's assistant held up her legs. Without speaking, Palladino pointed to more marks, more bruises on her thighs. Still holding her legs, the assistant looked at Palladino. Almost whispering, he said, "A guy could do a lot. . . ."

Moments later Scaring, Friedgood, and Hudock returned. "Doctor," Scaring was saying to Hudock, "we would like to take a sample of the organs back to Nassau County for toxicological examination—"

"They're trying to railroad me," Friedgood broke in. It was the second time, Palladino noted, Friedgood had become angry. "No parts of my wife's body are going to leave."

Again Meddis got on the phone to Lukash. This time he put Hudock on the line. "Friedgood thinks you're trying to railroad him," Hudock said into the phone. "We'll do the tests here."

"But, Doctor—" Scaring interrupted.

"I said we'll do the tests here."

/ v

It was dark when they left Saint Joseph's Hospital. A light rain was falling as they drove out of Hazleton onto Route 81 and headed north toward Route 80. Palladino drove. Meddis again sat beside him. In the back seat Scaring was asleep.

If Friedgood had been telling the truth when he said that he had kissed his wife good-bye on Wednesday morning, then Palladino would have to get hold of the maid, Lydia, who was the last person in the house with her mistress when she was alive. But if he was lying, if his wife had died the night before, as the autopsy seemed to show . . .

21

AT NINE O'CLOCK THE NEXT MORNING, STEVE Scaring burst into the office of the Nassau County medical examiner, Leslie Lukash. "This is what we have, Doctor," Scaring began. "We have Dr. Friedgood signing the death certificate and listing cause of death as a stroke. But we have an autopsy finding no cause of death. We have Dr. Friedgood saying he saw his wife alive at nine o'clock in the morning. But we have a corpse with a full stomach from the night before. We have bruises and marks Friedgood says were postmortem but which are clearly antemortem. And we have a hick coroner in Pennsylvania doing the tissue samples."

Leslie Lukash looked up from behind his desk. He had white hair and a benevolent expression. He wore a brown summer suit, a short-sleeved white shirt and silk tie. He lived, and worked, as meticulously as he dressed. He rose each day at six. He was at his office each morning by eight. He was home every afternoon by four. He was in bed each night by ten.

Leslie Lukash did not particularly care for Steve Scaring. Scaring was too young, too ambitious, too cocky. Already

Lukash suspected that if they could find a case in Sophie Friedgood's death, Scaring would try to take credit for the investigation—no matter how much Lukash's work as a pathologist contributed to the break.

What disturbed Lukash was how little respect there was for forensic pathology, even among the medical profession. Certainly as county medical examiner he would never make the money most doctors on Long Island did. Of course, the Long Island doctors could say of him that he would never suffer from their stresses or have their expenses. Not the least of his advantages, they would say of him cynically, was that he had no need of malpractice insurance.

But the public did not understand his job, either. It was only partly in jest that the homicide dicks and the cops who drove the morgue wagon called him "ghoul." Those who knew their way around the morgue had seen his prize, his "museum," in which he kept the grimmest, grossest deaths and horrors. In formaldehyde were fetal monsters—babies with two torsos, four arms, two heads. A child who had been asphyxiated when he caught his neck between the bars of his homemade crib. A teenager who had been strangled, while masturbating, by a window-shade cord he had tied around his neck.

There were the threats, too. Over the years Lukash had been threatened by relatives of people whose bodies he had autopsied, who viewed his job as something indecent, inhuman. Orthodox Jews, who consider an autopsy sacrilegious, had protested at the morgue. A group of blacks had charged him with racial discrimination after he insisted on autopsying a young black man found alone and dead in a nearby motel.

Lukash was fifty-five years old, and had been the county medical examiner for eighteen years now. In that time he had moved the office into a new $3-million building adjacent to the county medical center. He had a full-time staff of forty-seven under him. He had also become something of a *bon vi-*

vant, enjoying, as *The Wall Street Journal* once described it, a cache of the finest pre-Castro Havana cigars.

He might not have made the money other doctors on Long Island did, but when it came to his work, his profession, he brooked no interference from any of them. "I know you. You were one of my students in Brooklyn," Palladino had heard Friedgood say to Lukash on the telephone in Fierro's Funeral Home the day before. Had Palladino been at the other end of the line, he would have heard Lukash's answer: "I don't know you. And I never was one of your students."

Now, this Friday morning in his office, young Steve Scaring said to him, "Doctor, can you call Hudock again? Can you persuade him to send us the tissue samples?" Lukash stared at Scaring. When he stared at someone, he gave the appearance of being asleep with his eyes open. He may not have cared for Scaring but he was intrigued. Later it would all become police work. Now it was still a pathologist's case. "What's the number?" he said.

Scaring waited while the call was being put through, wondering how Lukash would handle Hudock.

"George, this is Dr. Leslie Lukash, chief medical examiner of Nassau County," the pathologist said in his official, almost patronizing voice. "Now, George, I know you are going to incur expenses. I think it inappropriate that you have put in all this time. Why not just send the samples here to Nassau? We can do it for free for you."

Listening to Hudock now, Lukash sensed the man's tone had changed since the day before. Hudock had lost some of his self-assurance, Lukash felt. Money was the reason, Lukash would say later. Hudock must have realized how expensive it would be to pay for the tissue analyses himself.

"But how will you pick up the samples?" Hudock asked.

"Just leave that to me, George," Lukash answered.

He hung up the phone and nodded to Scaring. Without a word, Scaring dialed police headquarters in Mineola. Two hours later Captain Meddis was on his way back to Pennsylvania in a police helicopter.

/ ii

That same Friday morning Tom Palladino drove out to the Friedgood home in Kensington, looking for Lydia Fernandez. But there was no answer at the front door. Palladino decided to walk around to a side entrance off the driveway and try again. To his surprise, a tall, well-built man with thick white hair and a tan complexion, in slacks and a sports shirt, opened the door.

"Yes? What can I do for you?" he said in a heavy Yiddish accent. He had a powerful voice, almost theatrical, Palladino thought. The man stepped outside and introduced himself as Sholem Cohen.

It was awkward. Palladino didn't know whom he was speaking to. He introduced himself. "I'm looking for Lydia Fernandez," he said.

"Everybody is still in Pennsylvania," said Sholem Cohen.

"Oh," said Palladino, nodding. "In Pennsylvania."

For a few minutes they talked in generalities—Palladino literally trying to get his foot inside the door.

"I'm a cantor," Sholem Cohen finally said.

"Oh, a cantor?" Palladino exclaimed. He wanted to put Cohen at ease—to get him talking.

"I come from Israel. I've come to sing for the High Holidays. I've only been here a few weeks."

"Really?" Palladino said. "Where in Israel are you from?"

"Natanya," he answered. "Outside Tel Aviv."

"It must be an amazing place."

Palladino wanted Lydia.

"You must have a lot of pride to come for the High Holidays. Where will you sing?"

"My cousin Charles, he told me he has lots of contacts. I

thought he was rich. He took me to many synagogues in Brooklyn." Then Sholem Cohen shook his head sadly. "What a beautiful woman. I'm here in this country such a short time. To experience such a terrible thing. You never met Sophie?"

Palladino didn't want to scare him. He sympathized. "No, unfortunately. But from what I heard in Pennsylvania, she was a wonderful person."

"Oh, you were in Pennsylvania?"

Now, Palladino had him curious. He could see Cohen saying to himself, Why the police? He could see Cohen wanted to ask him questions.

"Why are we standing here?" Sholem Cohen said suddenly. "Come inside. I'll make you a cup of coffee."

Round one to Palladino.

They stepped into the kitchen. Palladino, whose pride was his home on a half acre in Huntington, was taken aback. Such a neglected house, he thought. The backyard with no patio. No place to entertain. The kitchen such an old kitchen. Not modern. Old lighting. Old faucets.

"Such a wonderful person," Sholem Cohen was saying. They were sitting at the kitchen table. "I was fortunate to have been able to spend some time with her."

He seemed very respectful of her. Palladino let him go on.

"I sat with her every morning. For three hours we would have coffee and breakfast together. Such a good heart. She was such a lonely woman. My cousin was never home."

"Oh?" Palladino let him go on. He wanted more. He still hadn't taken out his notebook.

"I never knew my cousin or his wife. This is the first time I ever met him. I knew his mother. She said he had connections. I thought he was rich. He took me to several synagogues. They were so small and old."

"Did you stay at the places you were looking to work?"

"Oh, no. Only here."

"You've been staying only here?"

"Yes. Except for one night. The night she died. I went to New York the night before, to my friend Cantor Aroni in Manhattan. For an interview for a job. It took so long I couldn't get home, so I stayed with him. I called all that night but got no answer. Early the next morning I called again. Charles answered the phone. I was surprised because I thought Lydia would answer. 'Sholem,' he said, 'where are you?' 'I'm in the city,' I said. He said, 'I thought you were in the next room, sleeping.' "

"What about the last time you saw her? Was she sick? Was she complaining of anything?"

"No, we were sitting and having breakfast. She had just won a golf match—the first match in a big tournament, she said. She was so happy. I was happy for her. She was crying, squeezing my arm. For a crippled woman to win a golf tournament . . ."

Wait a minute, Palladino thought. A cripple? What kind of cripple? Nobody had said anything to him about her being crippled.

"You know, it is not right for me to say anything about my cousin. He is good to me. I am a guest. He lets me sleep in his home."

Palladino backed off. He didn't want to ask him a head-on question. He couldn't believe he was in the house at all.

"Such a wonderful person. So many troubles . . ."

Uh-oh, thought Palladino.

"Because of her sickness?"

"No, no. They had arguments. Such arguments. Terrible, terrible arguments. I don't see a happy home here."

Bingo!

"It was a big family. A lot of problems with the children. She used to sit and talk to me and tell me all the different things. On Friday nights she sat at the table with the candles. She always wanted her family together. She wanted everything to be right. But my cousin was never home. He doesn't call. He doesn't come. She asks where he is. He doesn't answer. He sits and reads the paper. She yells and throws things. She would get very excited. Then he would get angry."

Sholem Cohen paused. He looked away from Palladino and said softly, "Once my cousin said he would kill her."

Now Palladino *knew* he wanted Lydia.

/ iii

They talked for two hours. Palladino decided to wait outside for Lydia and left the house. A woman was sitting in a parked car in front of the house.

"Hello, how are you?" she said to him.

She was, Palladino thought, very attractive. He gave her a big smile.

"Beautiful day," she said. She was waiting for the family. "I saw you in Pennsylvania," she said to him. "You're with the police?"

Was she Lydia? He hoped, he hoped.

"I'm Jack's mother," she said. "Jack Cook. He's married to one of the daughters."

She stepped out of her car. "Such a lovely woman," she said. "Strange. . . ."

As they were talking, the first of two cars pulled into the driveway. One was a station wagon. The other was a white Cadillac. A small, olive-skinned woman stepped out of the station wagon.

Palladino made for her. Two young women were with her. One, he saw, was a blonde, pretty, her long hair down her back.

"Excuse me, I am looking for Lydia Fernandez."

As he spoke, the small, dark-skinned woman walked over to him.

"Why do you want to speak to me?" she said. She was

wearing a black dress, Palladino noticed. The other two women were also wearing black.

Palladino wanted to get Lydia out of there. The family was gathering its forces. Palladino could see Friedgood now at the front of the house. He was walking toward them, upset. Palladino saw he wanted to get to Lydia. The blond girl saw it, too. Palladino was standing at the curb. I'm no schmuck, he told himself. He knew he had to make Lydia come to him to get her out of there.

"Well, you know she doesn't speak English," the blond girl said. "I'm an attorney."

Who was she? Palladino wondered. Why was she sticking so close to Lydia?

"I'm Esther. Dr. Friedgood is my father. I want the right to come," she said. "I speak Spanish. Where are you taking her?"

"To speak to the district attorney."

"I want to come along."

Palladino wanted Lydia out of there before Friedgood realized what was happening. While Esther went to get her pocketbook, Palladino led Lydia to his car.

/ iv

It was afternoon when Meddis arrived in Hazleton, at a small landing field outside the city. A Hazleton police officer was there to meet his helicopter and drive him to Saint Joseph's Hospital. At the hospital, Meddis noted in his date book, he received samples of tissue from Dr. Hudock—one container of bile, 20 milligrams of blood, 250 grams of brain tissue, 80 grams of kidney, 200 grams of liver—plus 200 cc's of stomach contents and 30 cc's of her urine. Each sample, he noted, was in a plastic container.

Meddis placed a gummed seal on each and wrote the date, 6/20/75, on it. He put all the containers in an insulated white container supplied by Hudock, closed the outside container with three gummed seals, and put his initials and the date on the seals. He then walked out to the hospital parking lot, where the Hazleton police officer was waiting to drive him back to the helicopter. In all, Meddis had been in Hazleton less than an hour.

22

AT AGE THIRTY-THREE, STEVE SCARING WAS THE
youngest homicide chief in the county's history, with a salary
of over thirty thousand dollars, an office in the west wing of
the county courthouse in Mineola, within walking distance of
police headquarters, and a car with a siren and flashing red
light. He had come a long way from his origins as the son of a
city cop named Scaringe, who had had to move his family all
over the county while Steve was growing up. Scaring had
changed the spelling of his name in college—during a "period
of growth," as he vaguely referred to it—so that it would be
more "distinctive."

Married to a detective's daughter—even that was a step
up for him—he had been working as a claims adjuster for All-
state Insurance, and had just passed the bar, when he decided
to join the Oyster Bay branch of the Republican Party. He
then approached his district leader about a job as an assistant
district attorney, and two days later he had an appointment
with the DA, Bill Cahn. The following week he was hired.

In the DA's office, under Cahn, Scaring throve. There
was no question that he had ability. Tall, dark, funereally thin,

his black hair combed meticulously in place, he appeared in the courtroom in somber three-piece suits that resembled mourning clothes. By no means was he a grandstander, like so many of his peers. No histrionics or perorations for him. He never raised his voice. He spoke with the utmost reverence for the proceedings about him. His was an onerous but necessary duty—that was the image he conveyed—a deathly serious business. No time for jokes or digressions, either in the courtroom or in his investigations, no time for Palladino's apples, pears, or oranges. He was far too cautious for that, and far too ambitious.

His break came three years later, in 1972, when he was a second assistant in the Homicide Bureau. There had been a murder in Valley Stream, on the South Shore, of the wife of a Brooklyn school principal; she had been given chloroform while sleeping beside her husband. The principal, detectives had learned, had been having an affair with a teacher at the school. The two of them had met with a self-described mobster named Frankie Vitale and discussed paying him $25,000 to arrange the death of the wife.

Yet the detectives were unable to discover who had administered the chloroform. And neither Cahn nor the Brooklyn district attorney, Eugene Gold, the man who had once defended Charles Friedgood, appeared interested in prosecuting the case. Scaring, however, volunteered. When the indictment was announced, it was suddenly front-page news.

It was the first big trial for him, and against the best in the area. The principal and his girlfriend had hired two of the best-known criminal-law attorneys, John Sutter and Abe Brodsky. Yet Scaring, half to his surprise, proved to be their equal. Once, during a court recess, Sutter and Scaring fell into conversation, and Sutter mentioned that each weekend he retired to his cabin in Connecticut to unwind. Scaring was secretly pleased—and each weekend, when Sutter went off to Connecticut, Scaring went home and pored over the case. His diligence paid off: when the two were convicted, Scaring's reputation was made.

Three years later Cahn, up for reelection, was defeated and was subsequently convicted of fraud and sent to jail. His successor, a Democrat who cared less for party affiliation than for performance, appointed Steve Scaring chief of Homicide.

Yet it had been a slow first year. There had been only one case of note, that of a young black woman who had shot to death her white lover, who was the clerk to a New York State Supreme Court Justice. But she had been declared incompetent to stand trial and in May of 1975 was committed to a mental hospital. There was no action there. So when Scaring was contacted by Meddis about stopping the burial of Friedgood's wife, he had been mildly interested. When he heard the report on Hudock's autopsy, he had begun to move. Now, on a Friday afternoon in June, he was sitting in his office waiting for the call from Palladino to say he had Lydia with him.

"She wants to come in with the daughter—Esther," Palladino told him when he called.

"So bring them both," Scaring said.

/ ii

Thirty minutes later they were in his office. What Scaring saw was a frail, middle-aged woman and a girl in a black dress—an aggressive young girl, he thought, perhaps too aggressive.

"I'm not going to let you speak to Lydia," Esther began.

"Why not?" Scaring said gently. "Tell me why. Talk to me instead."

Besides gaining a reputation from the school principal's murder trial, Scaring had gained something else. Watching Sutter during the proceedings, he had been struck by how, as he put it, "he adapted to each particular event, how he related to each particular witness." He would never forget Sutter's questioning of the state's chief witness, the hood Frankie Vitale, who had testified about the $25,000 offer he had received from the school principal and his girlfriend to murder the wife.

After sizing up Vitale on the witness stand—a large, fat, unkempt man whose open-neck sports shirt revealed the gone-to-seed body of a heavy drinker—Sutter had approached him casually, slouching beside him for a moment. Then, companionably, evenly, as though to put him off his guard, he had said, "Hey, Frankie, how ya doing? I'm Johnny Sutter."

This Friday afternoon in his office, Scaring remembered how Sutter had met his witness on the witness's own terms and struck exactly the right note. He sensed that the Friedgood girl's aggressiveness came from fear. But what was she afraid of?

The rule book said that in every murder case you look first for a lover, second for money problems. So in a tough, offhand voice that matched Esther's, and implied he had routinely seen such cases and asked such questions, Scaring said to her, "All right, Esther, we're going to get around to it sooner or later. Was your father having an affair?"

"Some would say he was," she answered him as nonchalantly as he had asked the question.

"Who was it?" he asked evenly, looking directly at her, struggling not to reveal in his expression or in his voice the surprise, the elation he was feeling about her response.

"His nurse. Harriet Larsen."

"Where is she now?"

"In Denmark, with the two children."

"Esther," he continued, still looking directly at her, still talking as though this were the most natural question he could possibly ask her, "did your father have any financial problems?"

"My father always had financial problems," she answered him. "He was always in debt. That is not important."

Suddenly the telephone rang. Scaring answered it. It was Esther's husband. Scaring turned to Esther.

"Why don't you take it in the other room, where you'll have more privacy?" he asked, smiling at her. He stood up and escorted her into his outer office, where Lydia was waiting. He waited for her to sit down, and when he heard her begin speaking on the telephone, he ushered Lydia into his office, then locked the door behind them.

/ iii

An hour later, when Palladino dropped Esther and Lydia off in Kensington, he noticed a bearded young man wearing sandals walking quickly across the front lawn toward him. In his hand was a piece of paper that looked like a file card. As he reached Palladino he suddenly struck out his arm and held open the card in his palm for Palladino to read.

Who is this jerk? Palladino asked himself. Then, looking at the card in the young man's hand, he read the words "I want to make contact with you." On the back were a name and a phone number. The name was "Avi."

23

THE NEXT MORNING, SATURDAY, TOM MANNING, Nassau's assistant toxicologist, arrived at the county morgue at eight A.M. Manning usually spent Saturday with his wife, examining prospective model homes out in Suffolk County off the expressway. But Lukash had called him late Friday afternoon, saying he wanted him there the next day for "a special case," as Lukash had termed it. "It's probably going to be negative," Manning remembered Lukash's saying to him. "It's a woman with a previous CVA history. But let's run it through, anyway."

When Manning arrived at the morgue, he was surprised to find Lukash waiting for him. Lukash never came in on Saturdays except when there had been a homicide. He handed Manning the Styrofoam container Meddis had delivered the day before. In it were a small plastic bag marked BRAIN; two plastic envelopes marked STOMACH CONTENTS; a plastic envelope marked LIVER; one marked KIDNEY; a plastic vial of bile; two vials of blood; and two containers of urine. Routinely, Manning would always take out his black Magic Marker and write the case number on any sample he was given. This case, however, was still technically Pennsylvania's. It had no number. So on each of these containers Manning wrote the initials SC—"special case." Though he could not know it at the time, it would be the most special case he had ever had.

As he did every weekday morning, he took the elevator to the third floor, where the toxicology labs were located. Since it was Saturday, the doors leading from the elevator to the labs were locked. He turned on the lights and unlocked the door to the main office, where the phone was located, so he could answer if an emergency toxicology request should come in. He then put on a white lab coat that flapped around his thin, lanky body, and pulled on a pair of rubber gloves. As he had done hundreds, perhaps thousands, of times before, he entered what was known as the grinding room; here he would prepare the samples marked SC for a series of tests to determine the presence of drugs or other foreign substances.

The testing routine, known as the Stas-Otto procedure—which is named after two German scientists and has been used by toxicologists since the turn of the century—requires first an examination of the samples of the brain tissue and stomach contents. Manning took a round-bottomed flask, opened the container labeled STOMACH CONTENTS, and poured some of the white, gelatinous-looking substance into the flask. He then added a pint of water.

He next took a pair of forceps, picked out some of the filmy red-and-white substance from the brain container, weighed it, put it into a Waring Blendor, added a pint of water, and turned the machine on. Twenty seconds later he poured this mixture into another flask. He then put both flasks, containing stomach contents and brain tissue, on a metal cart.

Next he took a bottle of urine and a vial of bile and placed them on the cart. He poured some of the blood sample into an empty test tube, and another portion into a test tube in which he had put some salt. He put rubber stoppers in both test tubes and placed them on the cart also. His samples were now ready for testing. His work in the grinding room was completed. It was nine A.M.

Manning pushed the cart down the corridor to what is known as the steam-distillation room, where he would run his first test on the brain tissue and stomach contents. He fitted each of the two flasks into a heating system and connected the openings of each, with tubing, to two empty flasks. As the original flasks heated, steam would rise from the liquid contents of each, forming a distillate that would be caught separately in the second pair of flasks. Each distillate would then be tested for the presence of alcohol (and, if found, the quantity), and the residue in each of the original flasks would then be analyzed in a series of other routine procedures that would continue over the next twenty-four hours. By then Manning would have completed his preliminary tests on the sample of Sophie Friedgood's other organs. The results of the tests on the brain tissue and the stomach contents would confirm what he had already found.

/ ii

While Manning waited for the steam distillation to finish, he took the bottle of urine and went to a corner lab. The lab faced north, and though it was only on the third floor, the land outside was so flat he could see out the windows to the North Shore hills in the distance.

The first test here was a simple one. Friedgood had told Palladino that Sophie had taken some Empirin Compound #3 that night. If she had, a quick test for salicylate, or aspirin—which with phenacetin, caffeine, and codeine constitutes Empirin Compound #3—would show its presence. Manning poured a drop of Sophie Friedgood's urine into a test tube. He then took a yellow substance, the same color as the urine, which is known as a Trinder's reagent, and poured it into the test tube. If the solution turned purple, the presence of aspirin would be indicated. Moments later a puzzled Manning had his first result. Taking a pen from his lab-coat pocket, he wrote, "Trinder's—negative." There was no evidence of Empirin Compound whatsoever.

Next he would proceed routinely to determine the presence of certain common drugs—opiates, amphetamines, barbiturates, and methadone. Here he was using a new test, only a few years old, involving a machine known as a gamma-ray counter, which counts the number of radioactive particles in solution. The first test was for opiates, and Manning set up four small, empty test tubes for the procedure. Into one, the test sample, he added two drops of Sophie's urine. From a standard toxicological kit in the lab, he took a few drops of a positive-opiate urine sample and placed it into two of the other test tubes. He did the same with a negative-opiate urine sample, placing it into the last test tube. To each of them he added four drops of radioactive solution, then four drops of a straw-yellow liquid antibody, which would indicate the presence of an opiate.

He repeated this procedure for the two other drug groups—the amphetamines and barbiturates—and for the methadone. He then shook each test tube—there were four for each drug, sixteen in all—and let them incubate for half an hour.

While he waited he began another routine procedure for any other drugs that might be in the urine. First he poured the urine into a test-tube-like instrument known as a separatory funnel. He then added a few drops of a buffer, a clear solution of ammonium chloride in ammonium hydroxide, to decrease the urine's acidity. To this he added two ounces of ether, which would extract any drugs from the urine. He then shook the funnel.

When he stopped, the ether and the urine had separated, the ether clear on the top, the urine yellow on the bottom. Any drug from the urine had now presumably passed to the ether solution. Manning took a beaker and poured the ether into it through a piece of filter paper. He then placed the beaker on a steam table, a steam-heated stove top with no flame. For ten minutes he let the ether heat, boiling the liquid off, so that only a brown residue would be left at the bottom of the beaker.

Meanwhile, as the ether boiled, Manning returned to his radioactive test. With all sixteen tubes incubated, he added another reagent, a clear liquid solution of ammonium sulfate, which turned each test tube milky white. He then took the test tubes and placed them into a large, boxlike centrifuge, with a top door and small holes for holding the tubes. He shut the door and turned the machine on.

Ten minutes later he opened the centrifuge door. In each test tube, clear liquid had separated from the milky white; the clear liquid had risen to the top and the milky-white precipitate remained at the bottom. After pouring off the liquid and disposing of the precipitate from each test tube, Manning placed the test tubes in the gamma-ray counter. For each drug the machine would produce four numbered readings of the radioactivity: the number for Sophie's test urine sample, the number for each two drug-positive urine samples, and the number for the drug-negative urine sample. Depending on which control sample—drug-positive or -negative—Sophie's test sample corresponded to, Manning could determine the presence or absence of each of the four drugs in Sophie's urine.

While he waited for the ray counter to do its work, he returned to the steam table. The ether had all boiled off and left brown residue in the bottom of the beaker. Manning added alcohol to turn the residue into liquid. He then took out a thin-layer plate of glass that was coated with a gel. With a delicate, needle-thin glass rod, he began transferring the liquid, drop by drop, to the bottom of the plate, where it formed a small brown spot.

Then, while he let the liquid dry on the plate, he turned back to the gamma machine. The radio counts were coming off. Barbiturates, negative. Methadone, negative. Amphetamines, negative. Opiates, positive. He looked again. Opiates, positive. His first thought was that it was codeine, from the Empirin. But the Trinder's reagent had been negative for Empirin, so it could not be Empirin at all. What was going on here?

He looked at his watch. It was noon. He had found the first positive result, but what did it mean? He would continue with his thin-layer chromatography tests for drugs. Perhaps if the results of those tests were consistent with the presence of an opiate, the significance would become more clear.

/ iii

An hour later, he began to think he had something. Taking the glass plate on which the spot of urine-ether concentrate had dried, he put it in a tank filled with a developing solvent and let it stay there thirty minutes. Soon a faint gray line, running horizontally through the spot on the bottom of the plate, began to appear. Gradually, increasingly visibly, the line began moving up the plate. With it, it carried the drug from the spot.

The more a certain drug takes to this developing solvent, the higher it moves up the plate. Methadone, for example, will move to the top of the plate. By determining how far up the plate a drug has traveled, one can determine which drug it is.

Within a few minutes a large spot had solidified about three quarters of the way up the plate. Below it, slightly more than halfway up the plate, was a smaller, fainter spot. From having done thousands of similar tests, Manning knew which drug stopped at that place. It was Demerol. Demerol was also consistent with the positive opiate finding from the radioactive test, for Demerol is a synthetic opiate.

But how much Demerol had Sophie Friedgood been given? Was it a lethal amount? The quickest, easiest organ to test for the presence of Demerol is the liver: one takes part of it, puts it in a solution, and runs it through an ultraviolet spectrophotometer, a machine that measures the amount of light that passes through a solution.

Manning returned to the grinding room and took the liver out of the refrigerator. It was in a bag, in two chunks, weighing altogether 200 grams. He ground up 50 grams of it in the blender, then poured it into a flask. He took the flask back into the corner lab and added ether. He shook the flask and watched the brown liver sediment drop to the bottom; the ether, yellowish and bright, was rising to the top. It would take at least an hour till the separation process was completed. Manning looked at his watch. It was now one-thirty. He decided to go to the hospital cafeteria and have his lunch.

An hour later he returned to the lab. He poured off the ether and added to it hydrochloric acid, which is clear and colorless. This was the solution he would run through the ultraviolet spectrophotometer. The amount of light the Demerol absorbed would tell the amount of Demerol in the liver. The absorption of the light would register on a graph, producing a kind of printout on a piece of paper.

Five minutes after he placed the solution inside the spectrophotometer, the printout appeared. On it Manning saw three high peaks and troughs. He had tested enough drugs in the spectrophotometer to recognize the configuration immediately. Merely glancing at the printout, he knew that the amount of Demerol in the liver was lethal.

By the time Manning had completed all his tests it was close to four o'clock. Lukash had gone home, and now Manning telephoned him to report his preliminary findings. It looked, he said, as if the death had been caused by an overdose of Demerol, probably by injection. Manning was puzzled. To a layman the tests he had just conducted might have seemed difficult, intricate. But to a scientist, to a doctor, they were the most mechanical, routine procedures. Demerol was so obvious, such an easy drug to discover. Any doctor would know that. If a doctor wanted to hide the murder of his wife, Manning thought, how could he have been so dumb?

24

AT FOUR O'CLOCK THAT SATURDAY AFTERNOON, Steve Scaring was sitting with his wife and eight-year-old son at his son's Little League play-off game. Scaring was the team's manager, and ordinarily he paid the greatest attention to each play. But every hour throughout the day he had been phoning Lukash at home to ask if Manning's test results were in, and his mind couldn't focus on the game. In between innings, shortly before five, he walked to a pay phone a few yards from the field and called again.

Minutes later, as his son's team came up to bat, he was feverishly calling the young assistant district attorney on weekend call for emergencies. "I want a search warrant prepared so we can look for Demerol and a hypodermic syringe at Friedgood's home," he said tersely. "I want it now. Go over to the Homicide Squad and get it started."

He hung up and fumbled for another dime in his pocket. From the field there were squeals and shouts. Someone had gotten a hit. He turned back to the phone and dialed Meddis' number. "Get hold of Palladino at home," Scaring shouted to him over the screams of the Little Leaguers and their parents. "I need him to draw up the warrant."

For a search warrant to be approved by a judge, it must clearly establish probable cause for the belief that the premises for which the search warrant is sought contain evidence of a crime. In this case, that meant Scaring had to show probable cause for his belief that a hypodermic syringe, needle, or bottle of Demerol would be found at Friedgood's house. The medical examiner's office had established that a crime appeared to have been committed—Sophie Friedgood had died as the result of an overdose of Demerol, probably administered by injection—but it would not be so simple to convince a judge that evidence of how this had happened remained at 47 Beverly Road.

Now, again between innings, Scaring rushed to the pay phone and called Homicide to check on their progress. By six o'clock Palladino had arrived at the squad room. But there were problems, he told Scaring. They couldn't seem to get a handle on it.

It was clear what the trouble was. The young assistant DA didn't know the case. Preparing a search warrant, Scaring knew, was like telling a story—with accounts from witnesses so the relevant facts are in sequence. But there were so many facts. So many details. They simply could not organize the story.

"Steve, it's not moving," Palladino said when Scaring called again. "We're still on the first page."

By now the game had gone into extra innings. Scaring looked at his watch. It was after six. Leaving his wife to manage the team, Scaring raced home, changed into a coat and tie, and raced off to police headquarters.

"What the hell is going on here?" he shouted as he barged into the room at seven-thirty. Palladino, the assistant DA, and Meddis, who had arrived just a few minutes before, were all there, in their street clothes, talking to themselves out loud, trying to organize the case in their minds. "We're having trouble getting it together," said Palladino.

"Give me a pad. Let's start writing it out," said Scaring. "On Wednesday, June 18, 1975, Sophie Friedgood was found dead in her bed," he wrote. "She was pronounced dead by her husband, Dr. Charles Friedgood, who signed the death certificate."

As he finished writing a page, Scaring ripped it off and handed it to one of the others to type. But he was not a writer. And they were not typists. Outside, it was beginning to grow dark.

Three hours later they had completed a six-page affidavit. Scaring felt he had enough to go on. Palladino put in a call to the district-court judge on weekend call. It was Raymond Harrington, a fairly strict law-and-order man, Scaring knew.

But it was not until midnight that Harrington arrived. With him was his secretary. The two of them sat down at one of the desks and began to read as the others stood and watched. But as they read, Scaring saw, they began whispering to each other. Finally Harrington stood up. "It's not enough. You don't have enough. Probable cause that he committed the murder is just not there."

He handed Scaring back the affidavit. Scaring stared at it. Harrington yawned. It was nearly one A.M. He was going home. They could call him there if they needed him again.

Scaring had to start all over. Sophie Friedgood had been found dead on Wednesday. Her husband, a doctor, had signed the death certificate, giving a CVA—cerebrovascular accident—as the cause of death. Tests showed she had died from an overdose of Demerol, which had been injected. Friedgood had a mistress. He had money problems. But that wasn't enough. What else? Scaring's mind was racing. Whom else had they interviewed? Esther, who had told them about Friedgood's nurse, Harriet Larsen. Lydia, who had said Friedgood kissed his wife good-bye that morning. Friedgood's own statement. Sholem Cohen. Scaring had forgotten about him. What had he said to Palladino? Sophie had lots of problems. Problems with the children, with her husband. Fights. They had terrible fights. She had shouted and thrown things. He had sat smiling and reading the paper. Once his cousin said he would kill her. . . . That was it! The fights! The threats!

"I think we've got it," he said softly.

It was nearly five in the morning when they finished typing. Palladino drove out to Harrington's house in East Rockaway and brought the affidavit with him. An hour later he called Scaring. Harrington had signed it.

It was now six A.M. Since they hadn't slept, they agreed they would wait until a few hours later to begin the search. They would all meet at 47 Beverly Road at ten A.M.

/ ii

Scaring, Meddis, Palladino, and six other detectives arrived in four unmarked cars. It was a warm, sunny day. Scaring, Meddis, and Palladino wore jackets and ties. They walked up the path to the front door and rang the bell. Esther answered the door.

"We'd like to speak to your father," said Meddis in his formal, official voice.

Then Friedgood appeared at the door. "We have a search warrant for your house," Meddis began. "An autopsy revealed a lethal dose of Demerol in your wife's body. We're looking for the Demerol and a hypodermic needle."

A young man appeared. It was Esther's husband. "I'm a lawyer," he said. "I want to read the search warrant." He took the warrant from Meddis and walked past him, to the front lawn, and began studying it.

Meddis turned to Scaring. "How long do I have to let him read it?" he said.

"You don't," Scaring answered. "He's not party to the search."

Meddis walked to the lawn. "All right," he said, "let's have it."

"I'm a lawyer," the young man repeated. "I want to read it."

Meddis ripped it from his hand.

Esther's husband stood speechless. Scaring, Meddis, and Palladino, with the six other detectives behind them, trooped into the house to the living room. Palladino took a printed card from his pocket and began reading Friedgood his rights. "You have the right to remain silent. Anything you say may be used against you as evidence in court. You have the right to an attorney. If you cannot afford one, one will be provided to you."

He put the card back into his pocket. "Doctor," he said, "would you please initial the card and sign the date?"

Friedgood ignored him.

Meanwhile Meddis organized the detectives into two two-man teams to search the downstairs rooms first. "We would prefer that a family member accompany each team of detectives," said Scaring to Friedgood. "We want to be as reasonable and as complete as we can, Doctor."

Friedgood joined the team of detectives who would search the rear of the house. He motioned to Esther to join the team for the front.

They had hardly begun the search when the front doorbell started ringing: visitors—relatives with friends—were arriving to be with the family while they sat *shivah* during the period of mourning. As each visitor arrived Palladino escorted him or her to the side porch, where Friedgood's other children were waiting. Meanwhile the other two detectives remained in the living room. When the detectives searching the rooms brought in an item, the detectives in the living room photographed and catalogued it.

In the noise and confusion—the relatives and friends arriving at the front door, the detectives walking back and forth through the house—no one noticed when Friedgood led Esther off to a corner of the living room and began whispering to her in Yiddish.

"Nein fershayst Yiddish [I don't speak Yiddish]," she whispered back to him. "Da bar ivrit [Do you speak Hebrew]?"

"Lo midabar ivrit [I don't speak Hebrew]," he whispered back.

For a moment he stood staring at her, as if deciding what next to say. Then, in a low voice, almost a whisper, in English, he murmured, "Upstairs! File cabinet! Bottle. Syringe. Top drawer."

Esther knew the file cabinet. All the children knew it was on the second floor, just inside their father's study. At the same time, she would say later, she heard her mother's voice warning her, warning her about what she was about to do.

But she did not listen to her mother's warning. With the detectives searching, cataloguing, photographing, with the visitors entering, no one noticed her beckon to Beth, who stood at the edge of the porch. No one noticed Esther walk over and whisper to Beth, "Run upstairs! In the file cabinet is a syringe and bottle. Papa wants them."

Beth began to shake her head. "I'm not going to do it," she whispered. Suddenly she began to sob.

For a moment Esther stared at her, as her father had at *her*, moments before. What she despised most in people, she would say later, was weakness.

Half aloud, she murmured, "I'll do it myself."

While the detectives remained downstairs, absorbed in their search, she slipped out into the hallway, down the hall, and up the back stairs. She walked quickly to her father's study. Looking behind her to make sure no one was coming, she opened the top drawer of the file cabinet.

Later she would say she did not know what she was doing or what she was thinking. She was so afraid. The police were so brusque, so rude. Her only thought was to protect her father.

Without looking, she reached into the top drawer of the file cabinet, feeling for the bottle and syringe. But there were two bottles there. She grabbed both, as well as the syringe, and put them in a brown paper bag that was lying in the drawer.

Again she turned to make certain no one was coming. She lifted her dress, stuffed the paper bag inside her underpants, and walked back downstairs.

/ iii

The search continued through the afternoon. Toba, who had been sitting on the porch with the others, was afraid to come inside. But she could see into the living room. She noticed Beth shaking, holding herself and sobbing.

Where was Esther? Toba wondered. As the detectives continued to search upstairs, she walked into the living room and up the stairs behind them.

Esther was standing in the hallway, following the detectives as they went from room to room. "Esther," said Toba, "why don't you relax? Go down to the porch and sit down. I'll stay here and keep an eye on things."

Esther shot Toba a look and shook her head. "No, no," she whispered. "I can't. I can't sit down."

"I don't understand," whispered Toba.

"Come over here," Esther whispered back. "I have to tell you something."

She led Toba into one of the bedrooms and closed the door. She pointed to her skirt. "I have something here and I can't sit down," she hissed through her teeth.

Toba shook her head. She still didn't understand.

"Swear you won't tell anybody about this."

"I swear," said Toba.

Esther reached under her skirt and pulled out the paper bag. She emptied the contents onto the bed. Toba stared at the two bottles and the syringe. One bottle, she noticed, was clear glass with the word "Carbocaine" written on it. It was about one-quarter filled and had a rubber stopper in it. The second bottle was of heavier glass, with a paper label on which were barely visible marks. Attached to the bottle was a syringe, with a hypodermic needle. The needle was very long, the syringe large and old. The measuring lines had been rubbed off; a small amount of fluid was visible.

"Papa told me to go upstairs and get the bottle and the syringe," Esther explained. "I wanted to help him. I put it in my skirt. The needle was sticking into my thigh. That's why I couldn't sit down."

It was like a game, Toba thought. It was like playing detective. When they thought no one was looking, they sneaked across the hall into their father's study. They took out his pharmacological dictionary and carried it back to the bedroom; then they looked up the word "Carbocaine." The description was in technical language but they could understand that the substance was a local anesthetic. If given in large dosages, the book said, it could be harmful.

"Are you sure we shouldn't hand this in?" asked Toba.

"No, no," said Esther. "You know I can't do anything with it now."

"Where are you going to put it?"

"I don't know, I don't know. I'll put it somewhere."

"Well, where?"

"I don't want you to know."

"Good. I don't want to know, either."

"Swear you won't tell anybody about this."

"I swear."

/ iv

Later that evening, after the search was completed and the detectives and the guests had all gone, the children tried to piece together all that had happened. They were sitting at the table having dinner, with their father and his mother beside him. Now, besides bewilderment, there was tension.

"Papa," asked Beth, "why would anybody be suspicious of Mommy's death?"

"I don't know," Friedgood answered, staring down at his plate.

"Papa, the detectives were talking about Harriet. Who would tell them about Harriet?"

"I don't know. Somebody told."

"But why would anybody be suspicious?" asked Toba. "Why would they come here with a search warrant?"

"I don't know," he repeated. He sounded annoyed. "That is their routine. That is their regular procedure."

"Papa, what *about* Harriet?" asked Debbie. "What will you do about Harriet?"

"I told you, she's done a lot of work for me, and I paid her. There is nothing more."

"Value for her services?" asked Avi.

"This was payment for her hard work."

"You told us you used Harriet for the Miller case, to lie for you on the witness stand," said Avi, more sharply than he'd intended. "That is what you told Sophie. This is what she said to Debbie and me. Why did you do that?"

"She is a very able woman and has helped me a lot. I was paying her for her cooperation in the Miller case. That is all."

"Papa, we're not fools," continued Beth. "Don't treat us as such. We have eyes, we can see what is going on. You can't just sit there and look us in the face and tell us Harriet is your loyal nurse when obviously she is something much more than your loyal nurse."

"These are not your problems," he said, glancing around the table at all of them. "Each of you has your own problems. This is none of your concern."

His glance rested on Avi. "You," he said, "you were the one who opened up the thing about Harriet. If it weren't for you—"

"Why did you swear on your mother's life?" Avi interrupted, trying now to keep his voice from shaking. "Why did you swear you had no involvement with Harriet in front of Sophie the day we came to visit you, when in fact Harriet told us she had two children by you? Why are you still denying this today in front of everybody?"

Friedgood stood up. He walked over to the chair in which Avi was sitting and shook his finger at him. "I've been holding this in a long time," he said tightly, as though trying to keep himself from shouting. "I want to let you know how I feel. I don't ever want you to quote me as to things I might have said when you never heard them directly from me!"

"Go ahead," Avi responded, surprised at how steady his own voice sounded. "Threaten me. There are many witnesses here."

"You're the reason it came out about Harriet!" Friedgood shouted. "I want to tell you in front of everyone how I feel."

"Are you finished now?" asked Avi. "Are you all done?" As he spoke he became aware that the room had become silent. All of them who had been sharply questioning their father—Beth, Toba, even Debbie—all of them looked away. He felt he had finally said what all of them had been afraid to say to their father. What even he had been afraid to say.

For the first time he sensed he was truly an outsider to this family. Yet at the same time he felt a sudden exhilaration. He could not stop himself from what he was saying. He felt he was avenging Sophie, whom he had loved. He was confronting her husband for her. Already he had made contact with Palladino. Now, he decided, he and Debbie would call Steve Scaring.

"First," he said to his father-in-law, "I tried many times before to get in touch with you. I have left messages with your answering service. You can call them and find out how many times. We—Debbie and I—talked to you directly in your office, asking you many, many times to come to our house and talk to us about these things with Harriet so there would be no rumors. And you did not come. We pleaded with you many times and you delayed. You talked about many other things except the facts. And finally, when you did come out with it, it was only when Debbie specifically told you on the phone, 'Papa, if you don't come, it will be your loss because we are going to tell Mommy all we know.'"

"Stop it, stop it!" Esther suddenly shouted at him, leaping from her seat. "Get out! Get out of here!" Her husband stood up to restrain her. She began pummeling him with her fists, struggling to get past him, to strike Avi.

"Papa," Beth said abruptly, "I want to know how Mommy died. What about the search? What about the needle? What about the Demerol they found in the autopsy?" she said, glaring now at Esther.

For a moment there was silence.

"What is Demerol?" asked Debbie.

"It's a painkiller," her father answered.

"Mommy didn't use Demerol, did she?" said Toba.

"Sure, sure she did," he answered. "She had a few drinks that last night in Lundy's. That and the Demerol together could have affected her.

"There were a lot of needles in the house," he continued, as though he had suddenly thought of something, an escape. "When I found your mother in bed, there was Demerol on her night table and under her pillows. I tried to get rid of it when I found the body. I threw it away. I wanted to protect your mother's name."

"Papa," said Beth, "are you saying Mommy committed suicide? You know Mommy would never have done that."

"Papa," said Toba, "are you saying Mommy was a drug addict?"

"She was injecting herself," he answered.

"I don't believe you," said Beth.

"But, Papa," continued Toba, "if she was taking Demerol, she probably got the prescription from you, since you were her doctor. She never went to another doctor because you always took care of her. You were her doctor; you would know."

"There were other doctors she saw."

"Other doctors?" said Beth. "Where?"

"Local doctors. In Great Neck. There were things I kept from you, to save her name. She had another life. For two years she was a drug addict. She had sciatica and lots of pain from her stroke. There was a needle I hid. She was taking pills. I threw them away after I saw the body, to protect the family name."

"But why did you change your story about the Demerol?" said Beth. "Why didn't you say anything before?"

"Papa," said Toba, "we love you and want to believe you. If this is so, it will all come out." Suddenly she stopped, as though she had discovered something. "But if it was suicide, as you say," she said slowly, as though thinking aloud as she spoke, "they would have found the needle. Lydia would have found it."

"Why don't you ask Lydia?" he answered.

"Lydia would have said."

"Ask her if she found a needle on the dressing table. Why don't you. Ask her when she comes in tomorrow morning."

Suddenly he stood up and left the table.

/ v

Later, after dinner, Esther led her husband to the bedroom where she had hidden the brown paper bag. She spilled the bottles and the syringe out onto the bed. They began to look at the items closely, more closely than she had done before with Toba. Now, for the first time, she held the illegibly labeled bottle up to the light. Now, for the first time, she could make out the faint, raised letters, the word "Demerol."

Without speaking, she put the bottles and syringe back

in the paper bag and walked to the bathroom. Closing the door so her husband could not see, she put the bottle and the syringe in the sink and turned on the water, washing off all fingerprints. Then, unknown to her husband, she walked up to the third floor, opened a closet door, and stuffed the bag into the side pocket of a coat that was hanging there.

A week later, even after she realized what the syringe and bottles had to mean, she clung to the belief that someone else—anyone else—could have killed her mother. She had her husband climb into the house through a basement window to show that an intruder—Toby Miller, perhaps—could have sneaked into the house while Lydia slept. At the same time she went to a Gypsy fortune-teller in New York to reassure herself that she had been her mother's favorite daughter, and was devastated when she was told she had not been. The following month, she claimed to have heard her mother's voice warn her she would have to pay for what she had done.

For after she hid the paper bag in the coat pocket in the closet on the third floor, Esther told only one person—her father. Three days later, when she went back to the closet to look for it, the paper bag with the bottle and syringe inside was gone.

25

TUESDAY MORNING, TWO DAYS LATER, SOPHIE'S mother, Rose Davidowitz, her sister Lillian, and her brother-in-law Sidney Klemow arrived in Kensington from Hazleton. Rose had come not only to sit *shivah* for Sophie but to gain access to a safe-deposit box Sophie had opened jointly with her at the Chase Manhattan branch in Great Neck. As they prepared to leave for the bank Friedgood asked to accompany them. Together, all four of them drove there.

Inside, Rose Davidowitz produced the key to the box. A bank official opened the vault and lifted out the box. It was big, two feet wide and three feet long, more like a foot locker than a safe-deposit box. As is customary when a safe-deposit box is to be opened, the four of them carried it into one of the small private rooms off the main vault and locked the door behind them.

They stood around silently as Klemow, the brother-in-law, opened it. The first thing they saw were three large manila envelopes. Beneath them were some smaller envelopes. Beneath *them* was another safe-deposit box.

Klemow opened this. When he lifted up the top, they

noticed a passport. All of them stared at the name on its cover: Charles Edward Friedgood. Sticking out between the pages was what appeared to be a card. Klemow pulled it out. It was a Valentine's Day card, with the word "Papa" written on it. Klemow opened the card. Inside it were a half-dozen snapshots. One of them was of a blond baby in the arms of Friedgood's mother, Chafke. Another was a photograph of a young, nude woman.

Klemow, Sophie's mother, and Lillian stared at one another, speechless. Friedgood's voice cut into the shocked silence. "These are my private possessions," he said calmly. He reached into the box, quickly gathered up the passport and photographs, and stuffed them into his pocket. He turned to Klemow and the others. "Sophie was holding them for me," he explained.

No one else said a word. Silently, they began to empty the remaining contents of the box, with Friedgood standing behind them. It was not until that evening, when they had driven back to Hazleton, that they opened the manila envelopes. Inside one of them was another, smaller envelope. On it, in Sophie's handwriting, was the word *nofke*, Yiddish for "whore." Opening the envelope, they discovered Harriet's letters.

/ ii

That same afternoon Toba began cleaning out her mother's belongings from her parents' room. She worked mechanically, trying not to think. She was rummaging through one of her mother's closets when she came upon a manila folder—shoved in the back—with the word *nofke* written on it. Inside the folder was a pad of yellow ruled paper. On it were what appeared to be notes written by her mother to herself. Instinctively, without thinking, Toba began to read.

"Charles," it began. And below it was the number 1.

1) I was the last to find out.

2) Everyone we know knows about her. You deceived no one but me.

The only nice thing out of this is I know I am not paranoid.

Everything all and more was true.

I imagined.

Suspected.

Complained about.

Cried about.

Was depressed about.

Feared!

1) You went to Denmark Aug, 1974 (Not to Arizona)

2) You had an affair with this girl not a casual flirtation.

8 years

67, 68, 69, 70.

71, 72, 73, 74.

You spent thousands of dollars on her. While you screamed constantly at me how much I spend.

3) Now I understand why you were not spending as much as you said on me or my house or my children. But on the whore and her trips and trips to see her.

4) All the time I loved you and it was easy to deceive someone who loves you and wants to believe you.

5) You gave her my quilt and everything else that was missing in our home. If you wanted to leave me that would have been kinder.

Charles, you picked her up at the airport and took her to her apartment.

6) You were with her every Saturday and Sunday.

7) You shopped with her and her children.

You must hate me to allow me to spend hours alone, waiting for you

looking for you and phoning everywhere
making thousands of phone calls
trying to find you
wasting my life like this
this I resent so much
So many hours.
Why
What did I do to you? to make you do this to me?

8 years ago I was only 40 years old! I could have made a life for myself also!

Why should you have two lives and I have none?

If you cared for this girl enough to plan and plan and scheme and cover up and spend so much money to go to the lengths you did.

Why?

Are you still living two lives? Am I still being left out of one of your lives?

You continued to do this to me for 8 years, Does doing this give you pleasure? Did you and the whore laugh about this? Do you feel good about deceiving me all these years?

Toba finished reading. Holding her breath with embarrassment over what she had just seen, she quickly put the papers back into the folder and hid them in the closet. Then she began to cry.

26

CHARLES FRIEDGOOD TOOK HIS PASSPORT FROM
Sophie's safe-deposit box on Tuesday morning. That afternoon
he drove to the office of E. F. Hutton in Manhattan with a letter over Sophie's forged signature authorizing the sale of
$50,000 in securities in her name. Then at the National Bank
of North America, he forged her signature again, giving him
access to another safe-deposit box in her name. The day before—without telling anyone—he had been to the Chase Manhattan branch in Great Neck, where Sophie had kept another
safe-deposit box in her own name. After first being refused entry, he forged her name on a set of papers, dating them prior
to her death. In all, besides at Chase Manhattan and the Na-
tional Bank of North America, he had closed Sophie's accounts
at Manufacturers Hanover, East New York Savings, and the
Harlem Savings Bank. The following morning, when he left
Kensington, he carried in a black leather overnight bag over
$600,000, from Sophie's safe-deposit boxes, in jewelry and ne-
gotiable bonds that she had held in trust for their children.

/ ii

At seven o'clock Wednesday evening the telephone rang at 47 Beverly Road. It was the last day of *shivah,* and Beth, Debbie, and Avi were at home.

Beth answered the telephone. Hearing her father's voice, she silently motioned to Debbie and Avi to go upstairs and pick up the extension. When they did, they heard Friedgood saying, "I've gone to the hospital for an electrocardiogram. I have a bad heart. I have to go away and rest a few days."

"But, Papa where are you going?" cried Beth.

"I don't want to say."

"Papa, we need you here. Please, at least give us an address."

"I'm sorry for the argument the other day," he went on, as if he hadn't heard her. "You know I wouldn't do anything to hurt Mommy. Tell Jack the keys to my car are in an envelope in the Holiday Inn at Kennedy."

"But, Papa—"

"I'll call you in a few days."

"Can't you tell us where you're going?" she pleaded.

"No, I can't say."

"Well, are you at the airport?"

There was a pause.

"No," he answered. Then he hung up the phone.

Silently, so that Beth would not see him, Avi slipped down the back stairs and out of the house. He did not take the car because he did not want Beth to hear him. Instead he began to walk. Fast.

At the edge of the village near the Kensington police booth is a telephone booth. Avi walked up to it and began dialing Steve Scaring's office number. Three, four, five, six times he heard the phone ring. There was no answer. Scaring had already left for the day.

There was a Nassau phone directory by the phone. Avi opened it and began looking for the name Scaring. There was only one.

/ iii

Steve Scaring was at home watching television with his wife and children when, shortly before eight o'clock, the telephone rang.

"I'll get it," Scaring said, and went into the kitchen to pick up the phone. "Hello?"

"Mr. Steve Scaring?" said the voice on the other end of the line.

"Yes?"

"Mr. Scaring, this is Avi Menashe. I think Chuck Fried-good may be leaving the country."

Scaring raised his eyebrows. "Why do you think so?" he said, his voice calm.

"We just received a call from him. He said he was going away for a few days because he has a bad heart."

"When was the last time you saw him?"

"This morning. He was not at the house to sit *shivah*."

"Did he say anything about not coming home, about going away?"

"No, he didn't say anything."

"Why do you think he is leaving the country?"

"We just received a call from him. He wanted someone to pick up his car from the Holiday Inn, which is near Kennedy Airport."

Scaring's voice quickened. "What was he wearing when you saw him last?"

"A suit. A gray suit."

"I'll call you back."

Scaring motioned to his wife to come into the kitchen.

"It looks like Friedgood may be running," he said to her. "I think he's at the airport and may be going to Denmark."

"Why don't you see if you can stop him?" said his wife, the detective's daughter.

/ iv

At eight-thirty the telephone rang at police headquarters in Mineola. It was Scaring. He wanted the chief of detectives, Ed Curran.

"He's gone for the day," said the officer at the switchboard.

"Can you get him at home?"

"No way."

"All right," said Scaring, "I want the detective duty officer. Who is it?"

"Inspector Robert Edwards."

Scaring knew Edwards. He was a twenty-five-year veteran. Scaring had worked on at least ten homicide cases with him. He was a pro.

"I can't give out his number. I'll call him at home," said the officer. "Give me your phone number."

/ v

Five minutes later the telephone rang again in Scaring's home. It was Edwards. Scaring wasted no time.

"Bob, we've got a prime suspect in a homicide case I think is trying to run—tall, thin, fifty-five years old, curly gray hair, glasses, wearing a gray suit. . . ."

Moments after he hung up, Edwards backed his car out of his driveway and headed north on Hempstead Turnpike to the Eighth Precinct, on Hicksville Road, the nearest police

precinct to his home. Five minutes later, he walked through
the front door and up the stairs to the squad commander's
office. In twenty-five years on the job, Edwards had been involved in dozens of homicide investigations. He never felt
panic or an undue sense of urgency. Sooner or later, he would
say when he retired, all investigations blend into one.

Despite what Scaring had said, there was no evidence
Friedgood was in fact at the airport. All they knew was that he
had said his car was at the Holiday Inn. Edwards' first phone
call was to the Holiday Inn to discover if Friedgood or a man
fitting his description had registered there that evening. He
had not.

Edwards then dialed Kennedy Airport's Port Authority
police.

/ vi

It was nine o'clock when Edwards' call came in to the Port Authority police building, just off the Van Wyck Expressway at
the entrance to the airport. For the PA police at Kennedy,
nine o'clock falls in the middle of their heaviest tour of duty,
when most of Kennedy's air traffic, which consists of foreign
carriers that depart in the afternoon and arrive in Europe the
following morning, are returning to Kennedy in the evening.
The call was taken by Walter Shepherd, a twenty-three-year
veteran of the PA police, who picked up the phone in the detectives' small second-floor office, where it was transferred
from the central switchboard.

"This is Inspector Robert Edwards of the Nassau County
police. What are the possibilities of determining if an individual is on a flight going overseas?"

"What is the basis of the request?" said Shepherd.

"He's a prime suspect in a homicide case."

Shepherd motioned to his superior, the commanding

detective sergeant, who was sitting across from him, to pick up the phone.

"This is Detective Sergeant James Goulding," he announced to Edwards. "Do you have a warrant?"

"No, this is just an inquiry."

"What is the basis of the inquiry?"

"He is the prime suspect in the murder of his wife."

"Where is the individual going?"

"We're not sure. We think he is going to Denmark."

"What is the airline?"

"We're not sure of that, either."

"What is the individual's name?"

"Friedgood. Charles Friedgood. Middle initial 'E' for 'Edward.' "

"F-r-e-e-d–g-o-d," Goulding wrote. Professionals though they all were, Friedgood's name had been misspelled.

"Can you give me a description?" Goulding asked.

"Fifty-five years old. Five-ten or -eleven. Curly gray hair. Wears glasses. Wearing a gray suit."

"It will be a while," said Goulding. "I'll call you back."

/ vii

Shortly after seven o'clock Wednesday night, a tall, lean man with curly gray hair, wearing glasses and a gray suit, stepped up to the ticket counter of British Airways at Kennedy Airport. Somewhat to the ticket agent's surprise, the man carried no luggage, only a small black leather overnight bag.

"Do you have space on a flight to London tonight?"

"Yes, we do," the agent answered. "As a matter of fact you can have your choice of three or four seats for yourself tonight."

"What time is the next flight?"

"Eight P.M."

"Are there any flights after that?"

"Ten P.M."

"Are they busy?"

"No. You're lucky to be traveling tonight—there are plenty of seats. You can stretch out anywhere on the whole plane."

"I'd like a one-way ticket on the eight-o'clock flight," the man said.

Because of the possibility of an airplane hijacking, ticket agents for British Airways are instructed to be on the lookout for anyone purchasing a one-way ticket with a non-British passport. "May I see your passport, please?" the agent asked.

The tall, lean man took his passport from his pocket and showed it to the agent. "I have business over there and I intend to stay awhile and don't know when I'll be back," he explained with a smile.

The ticket agent studied the passport, issued to a Dr. Charles Edward Friedgood and dated January 24, 1973. Since it had been issued, the ticket agent noted, Charles Edward Friedgood had already been to Denmark and back.

A doctor, the agent thought. You could always trust a doctor. Without a word he handed the passport back to the man, who paid for his ticket with a Master Charge card.

Routinely, the ticket agent then checked the card through the computer, to make certain it was not a lost or stolen one. Moments later the computer screen came back empty. The ticket agent then issued a ticket to Friedgood for flight 500, due to depart at eight o'clock.

/ viii

"Walter, you and your partners begin calling the foreign carriers that fly direct to Denmark," Goulding called to Shepherd as he hung up on Edwards. In a book on the desk was a list of Kennedy's numbers for the different airlines' security police. Shepherd and his partner, Claude Haynes, began calling.

Scandinavian Airlines. Finnair. KLM. "We're looking for a Dr. Charles E. Friedgood," began Shepherd. "Fifty-five years old, tall, thin, five-ten or -eleven, wearing glasses and a gray suit. He is wanted as a prime suspect in the murder of his wife. We have reason to believe he may be leaving the country for Copenhagen tonight on one of your planes."

"We'll have to check. Give us a few minutes," was the answer. 'We'll call you back."

"We're looking for a Dr. Charles Friedgood," said Haynes. "Fifty-five years old, tall, thin, five-ten or -eleven, wearing glasses and a gray suit. He is wanted as a prime suspect in the murder of his wife."

One by one the calls came back. Scandinavian. Finnair. KLM. They had no record of a Charles Friedgood buying a ticket on any direct flight to Copenhagen.

They began calling the airlines with connecting flights to Copenhagen via London. Pan Am. TWA. British Airways. "We're looking for a Dr. Charles E. Friedgood. We have reason to believe he may be leaving the country for London tonight on one of your planes."

Then, at ten minutes to ten, Shepherd got a return call from British Airways Security. "We got a possible," he shouted out a moment later.

But there was a problem. The spelling was not the same. The airlines, they all knew, were reluctant to give out any passenger information to the police or to anyone else. British Airways wanted confirmation of the spelling before they would reveal the man's flight number.

Goulding put in a call to Edwards at the Eighth Precinct in Nassau. Moments later Shepherd was on the phone again to British Airways.

"Friedgood. Charles Friedgood. Middle initial 'E' for 'Edward.' Friedgood. F-r-i-e-d-g-o-o-d."

"There's a Charles Friedgood on the ten-o'clock flight to London," said British Airways Security. "Flight five-ten. He was also on the eight o'clock flight—five hundred—but he failed to show up. They're just closing the ticket counter at gate two. They're buttoning up the flight."

"Go!" shouted Goulding to Haynes while Shepherd remained on the phone. Haynes raced down the stairs. He grabbed the first detective he saw, and the two of them ran to an unmarked Port Authority car parked outside. Haynes jumped into the driver's seat. He turned on the red flashing light and his siren and shot off onto the Van Wyck Expressway, heading toward "terminal city," where the airline passenger gates are located.

British Airways is past the western edge of the main terminal, the International Arrivals Building. Haynes raced past it. At the western end, he shot onto the TWA entrance ramp, past where the planes leave their gates and taxi out onto the runway. Haynes swung sharply left. His red light flashing, his siren whining, he headed past the blue lights of the ramp on his left, past the white lights of the inner taxi field on his right.

Minutes later he could see the British Airways terminal in the distance. Suddenly a huge plane lumbered before him, across his path. A British Airways plane was moving out onto the inner runway a mile away into taxiing sequence. It was too far away. He was too late.

In desperation he looked toward the runway the big plane was making for. It was a clear night and he could see that two planes were ahead of it, waiting to take off. "Plane has left gate," he called into his police radio to Port Authority headquarters. "It's taxiing onto the runway."

Back at headquarters, Goulding summoned a patrolman at the front desk. The patrolman picked up a black phone on the wall. Above it in green were the letters KIA and, next to them, the words TOWER DIRECT—Kennedy International Airport's direct line to the control tower.

"Would you get hold of British Airways flight five-ten?" Goulding said to the tower. "See if you can get him back to the gateway. There is a murder suspect aboard."

In his car on the ramp, Haynes saw in the distance that

the plane had stopped, as all planes do just before they pick up speed for takeoff. But suddenly the plane was turning around. It was taxiing back past him, toward the gate.

"Report to gate two. Plane has been stopped," Haynes heard over the car radio.

He sped to the gate. The plane had stopped there. The car squealed to a halt and he jumped out.

There was an outside ramp up to the plane. Goulding was standing there with a security man from British Airways. The three of them climbed up the ramp and entered the plane.

They had been given Friedgood's seat number, in the front of the plane. There, in the fourth row, they spotted him—an older man, with curly hair, wearing glasses and a gray suit.

"Are you Charles Friedgood?" said Haynes.

"Yes," he answered.

"Can I see some identification?"

He took out his passport. "Friedgood, Charles Edward," Haynes read.

"Would you come with me, please?" said Haynes.

"Is it the thing in Nassau?" said Friedgood.

"Yes. Yes it is."

"All right," said Friedgood, standing up. He picked up his black overnight bag from between his legs and with the three policemen walked off the plane.

Epilogue

ON AUGUST 5, 1975, CHARLES FRIEDGOOD WAS arrested and charged with murdering his wife and looting her estate of nearly $600,000.

Three weeks before, after finding Sophie's notes to herself, Toba had gone to the police and confessed that Esther had hidden the syringe and bottle of Demerol. That night, police came to the Friedgood home and picked up Esther. For three hours she was questioned by Scaring at a police station house. In return for Scaring's dropping charges of concealing evidence and obstructing justice, which would have led to her disbarment, she agreed to testify against her father.

In October 1976 Charles Friedgood went on trial for murder in Nassau County. His children testified against him. On December 15 he was found guilty.

In January 1977 he was sentenced to prison for the maximum term, twenty-five years to life.

The following year the New York State Legislature passed a bill prohibiting doctors from signing death certificates for relatives. The bill is popularly known as "the Dr. Friedgood Bill."

/ ii

Five years after Sophie Friedgood's murder, Debbie and Avi still live in New York. Recently Debbie's picture appeared in the *New York Post* with that of the Jewish writer for whom she still works as a secretary, and whose name she does not want to reveal because, she says, "I do not want to connect him with the shame of my family."

At the trial she testified against her father, describing his relationship with Harriet; how the little boy Heinrich called her father "Papa"; how her father had told her at her apartment that he was planning to leave her mother; and how the day after her mother's death her father had refused to agree to an autopsy.

At the end of her testimony she looked up and noticed her father scribbling questions for his attorney to ask her, in order to trap her. Suddenly she burst into tears and ran from the courtroom.

/ iii

Toba lives on the West Coast, where she teaches English and where her husband, Larry, works with juvenile delinquents.

Beth lives in New York State with her husband, who has completed his residency. Recently she had a baby daughter. She named her Sophia.

David, the eldest son, is an osteopath in the Midwest. He did not testify at the trial, nor was he asked to. Recently his wife give birth to a baby daughter. They also named the child Sophia, but David has changed his last name.

Stephen, the youngest, testified against his father, but only at the last moment, after having at first refused to cooperate. More recently he dropped out of medical school in the Dominican Republic and returned to the United States. "I'm still confused," he said after his father's conviction. "I don't know what to believe. What would you believe if it were your father?"

/ iv

Esther and her husband have moved to the South, where they both practice law. She claims she has since spoken to her dead mother. "You may not believe this," she says, "but when Toba called the police to inform on me I was taking a shower and I could hear my mother uttering a loud cry from far away, warning me I would be in a lot of trouble.

"Why did I finally testify against my father? The Talmud says that if there are two people on a desert and only one drop of water to keep one person alive, even if one person dies, the other should take it. Why destroy myself? What more could I do for my father?"

Now, says Esther, she realizes just how like her mother she is. "I am strong. I don't tolerate weakness either in myself or my husband. Now my husband and I devote ourselves to luxuries. We have built a beautiful home. I buy beautiful tiles and beautiful wallpaper. We live on a golf course. We are always at the beach. We have a vegetable garden. We have a euphoric, a fantasy kind of existence. I want to enjoy my life. I want to enjoy every minute I have."

Recently she and her husband had a baby daughter. They also named her Sophia.

/ v

As for the others, Tommy Palladino won the Nassau County Police Department's second-highest award for his detective work on the Friedgood case.

Dr. Leslie Lukash is still the Nassau County medical examiner.

After the conviction, Steve Scaring went into the private practice of law, and now he is considering running for district attorney. He and Lukash barely speak.

/ vi

On a brisk fall day in 1977, an attractive, well-dressed woman in her late thirties arrived at Kennedy Airport from Copenhagen. She wore a wool suit; her hair was fashionably coiffed and lightened, and swept back over her ears. A man was there at the airport to meet her, to drive her one hundred miles upstate to a prison.

For the next seven days she rented a room at a nearby motel. During the day, always in her best clothes, her hair styled, her face carefully made up, she sat with Charles Friedgood in the prison's common room, which during the week is empty of visitors—just the two of them in the large, empty room. When no one was there she touched him, held his hand, embraced him. But when anyone—even a stranger—approached, she pulled back. Watching them together, one might almost have thought they were strangers.

Since that visit Harriet Larsen has returned to the United States regularly. It is not known how she pays for her plane fare, her clothes, her motel rooms, or her payments to Friedgood's lawyers.

Though the lawyers have told her to remain in Denmark, to stay out of sight, she does not hesitate to speak to anyone who she thinks can help her, to say that Charles Friedgood is innocent. "Why are they trying to ruin him?" she says one afternoon as she sits with Friedgood in the prison. "He wrote me letters, praying to God this nightmare would soon be over. He asked me to destroy the letters but I kept them. I saved them because they must prove something. No one could write letters like that unless he was innocent.

"Those needle marks," she explains, "why, of course she injected herself. Charlie couldn't have done it," she adds, staring at him. "She must have done it herself. This man is the most decent human being I have ever known."

/ vii

Nearly a year after his sentencing, on November 6, 1977, an article appeared in the New York *Daily News*. The headline was FRIEDGOOD FOUNDS CLINIC FOR PRISON'S AGED.
It read:

> Dr. Charles Friedgood, 59, once wealthy Nassau surgeon who was convicted of killing his wife to run off with his mistress, has used his medical skills to set up a pioneering clinic in prison for the elderly and handicapped.
>
> His efforts to help "forgotten people" in the Fishkill Correction Facility in Beacon have brought new purpose to the lives of many. In large part this is because he has weaned all of the 250 prison patients off the prescribed drugs that used to be the main force in their lives.
>
> A dozen former patients whom he treated before his imprisonment regularly travel from Brooklyn to bring him the fruits and vegetables they know he craves.
>
> Many of the former patients testified at Friedgood's trial in his behalf—and their regular pilgrimage provides the makings for the salads the physician tosses up and serves to the prisoners. . . .
>
> "Why should I be dragged down by an injustice that was done me? I'm doing the best I can to adjust." And one of the biggest physical adjustments has been the robust physical schedule of calisthenics and jogging he regularly keeps.
>
> "I never jogged before," he said. "I was always too busy to walk. My treatment of other forgotten people has given me an added purpose for living."
>
> Indeed his one principal purpose now is in the main-

tenance of the burgeoning unit he envisioned while he was housed in the maximum security prison at Dannemora.

While there he wrote a letter to the Correctional Service News that proved to be the turning point in his prison life and also proved to be a boon to the scores of elderly and handicapped prisoners who Friedgood believed were left to founder in a prison system that offered them nothing.

"The forgotten man in today's correctional facilities is the senior citizen, the prisoner who is over fifty years of age," Friedgood wrote.

"There are no programs for the rehabilitation of older men. . . . He can't communicate with the youth around him. His styles, tastes, mores and ideas are of a past generation. It is much more convenient for him to withdraw, to sit in his cell and dream of the past."

Friedgood painted a poignant picture of the aging prisoner condemned to inactivity, too embarrassed to try individual athletic pursuits and unable to compete in group sports. Such men are often humiliated by others and taunted with jeers that they are "old men," Friedgood said.

"Idleness and sedentary living accelerate the degenerative diseases and senility," Friedgood wrote. "Those inmates become aged, looking well beyond their chronological age. Present medical knowledge has proven that both physical and mental exercise is conducive for maintaining good circulation in the human body."

As a result of his ideas, he was moved to the medium security facility at Beacon where he set up the physical rehabilitation clinic to serve the state's aged prisoners. . . . It serves prisoners from all 33 state facilities.

By far the most significant achievement, Friedgood said, is his transformation of the treatment accorded older prisoners, taking them off the drugs and changing their diets.

"Not one of the 250 patients here who formerly survived on drugs is using drugs anymore," he said. "Their blood pressure is down and they live more useful lives, partaking in prison programs where they just used to lie in bed."

The physician regularly lectures prisoners on topics ranging from mental hygiene to venereal disease and birth control.

/ viii

Two blocks from Interboro Hospital in Brooklyn, on Crescent Avenue—a crumbling street of two-family homes and vacant lots—is a basement doctor's office. The door to the office is answered by a small, dark woman in a white nurse's uniform. It is Lilli Ruiz. She has been working there for more than a year.

Outside the office stands a white sign with the names of three doctors: Samir K. Dutta, MD; Gregorio Alvior, MD; and Byung Lim, MD.

Dutta says he has never met Charles Friedgood. He has taken over Friedgood's practice but he has not paid him anything for it. Dutta says he treated some of Friedgood's surgery patients who had come to him with postoperative complications. After Friedgood was sent to jail, Dutta wrote to him, asking to take over his practice until his release. Should that occur, Dutta stipulated, he would return Friedgood's practice.

"To make the patients feel at home," as Dutta puts it, he has placed another name on the white sign outside the office. Above the names of the three doctors is that of Charles E. Friedgood, MD.